Putting Citizens First

Engagement in Policy and Service Delivery for the 21st Century

Putting Citizens First

Engagement in Policy and Service Delivery for the 21st Century

Evert A. Lindquist, Sam Vincent and John Wanna (eds)

Australian
National
University

E PRESS

ANU
E PRESS

Published by ANU E Press
The Australian National University
Canberra ACT 0200, Australia
Email: anuepress@anu.edu.au
This title is also available online at http://epress.anu.edu.au

---

National Library of Australia Cataloguing-in-Publication entry

Title: Putting citizens first : engagement in policy and service delivery for the 21st century / edited by Evert Lindquist, Sam Vincent and John Wanna.

ISBN: 9781922144331 (paperback) 9781922144348 (ebook)

Series: ANZSOG series

Subjects: Public administration.
Public administration--Citizen participation
Public administration--Technological innovations.
Electronic government information.
Political rights.
Public interest.

Other Authors/Contributors:
Lindquist, Evert A, editor.
Vincent, Sam, editor.
Wanna, John, editor.

Dewey Number: 352.46

Cover design and layout by ANU E Press

Contents

Part I. Setting the Scene: The evolving landscape for citizen engagement

Part II. Drivers for Change: Innovations in citizen-centric governance

Part III. Case Studies: Land management and Indigenous empowerment

Part IV. Case Studies: Fostering community engagement and connectedness

Part V. Case Studies: Engaging with information technology and new media

John Wanna, Series Editor

Professor John Wanna holds the Sir John Bunting Chair of Public Administration in the Research School of Social Sciences at The Australian National University and is director of research for the Australia and New Zealand School of Government (ANZSOG). He was also until 2012 Professor of Politics and Public Policy at Griffith University, and formerly principal researcher with the Centre for Australian Public Sector Management and the Key Centre for Ethics, Law, Justice and Governance at Griffith University. Professor Wanna has written numerous monographs, including two textbooks on policy and public management. He has produced a number of research-based studies on public management including: *The Reality of Budget Reform in the OECD* (2010); *Comparing Westminster* (2009); *Westminster Legacies: Democracy and responsible government in Asia and the Pacific* (2005); *Yes Premier* (2005); *Controlling Public Expenditure* (2003); *From Accounting to Accountability* (2001); and, *Managing Public Expenditure* (2000). In 2009 Professor Wanna completed a study of service delivery in the Australian Government entitled *Policy in Action: The challenge of service delivery*. His most recent authored book, produced with Tracey Arklay, is *The Ayes Have It: The history of the Queensland Parliament 1957–89* (2010), a major legislative study of historical significance. Professor Wanna has held many Australian Research Council grants over the years, but also conducts research independently and through ANZSOG. His research interests include Australian and comparative politics, public expenditure and budgeting, and government–business relations. His political commentary has appeared in the *Australian*, *Courier-Mail* and *Canberra Times* and on Sky News as well as ABC radio and TV. The ANZSOG ANU E Press series, which he edits, is now approaching 40 titles. See <http://epress.anu.edu.au/titles/australia-and-new-zealand-school-of-government-anzsog-2>

Foreword

Allan Fels

This volume of essays brings together leading academics and practitioners from Australia, New Zealand and beyond to express current developments and explore future directions in citizen-focused government. Drawing on their varied research and experience on the ground, experts in the field — often with international backgrounds — use their contributions to explore actual experiences and applications.

Since the Australia and New Zealand School of Government (ANZSOG) series began in 2005 it has focused on providing thought-provoking, relevant and practical content and pushing agendas pursued by governments both here and overseas. The 2011 edition is no exception. Several major themes underpin this volume of essays; themes introduced by Professor Evert Lindquist. But, from my perspective, citizen engagement is one of the most confronting, demanding and exciting challenges to which governments have committed themselves. It suggests that we need to develop new cultures; that we must operate not in the traditional 'business as usual' mode; that we must relax our preoccupation with command and control approaches. It also implies that we must invest more time and effort to achieve results and be prepared for the long haul — achieving engagement is a long-distance commitment, not a sprint, and the necessary attributes are those of Australia's 2011 Tour de France champion Cadel Evans, rather than Jamaica's sprint sensation Usain Bolt.

So, we at ANZSOG aim to cover a number of related themes in this volume — which build on each other and develop the various agendas we need to marshal. We will examine how policy actors (designers and implementers) can:

- work across departments and across levels of government to better meet citizen and community needs
- assemble and better utilise citizen feedback and incorporate citizen satisfaction into improved service delivery
- engage with citizens to improve policy design and implementation, entrusting them with input into policy initiation and formulation
- customise services to ensure citizen and community needs are met, allow more choice and personalised tailoring.

We live in an era where governments cannot act in isolation, where community disaffection with government is, arguably, prevalent and where new communities are increasingly forming and evolving online. Governments do not know all the answers — and the community does not believe they do. Consequently, questions about how to involve citizens and share learning become ever more pertinent. Recent policy experiences (such as with the Northern Territory Intervention or the planning for the Murray Darling Basin) have highlighted the importance of community-centric and locally generated solutions rather than top-down, universally prescribed approaches. Governments and community face an equally steep learning curve in addressing this issue.

But, once we start down this track and heighten community expectations about being listened to, other significant issues will emerge. For instance:

- What does citizen-centric really mean? And who gets to define or shape it over time?

- Is citizen engagement merely code for governments thinking about improving the alignment between what they wish to achieve and what the community will accept; or does it entail a more radical set of approaches where the community actively drives policy designs and policy processes?

- What are we engaging about? Are we creating *options* and looking for *innovations*, consulting on *applicability* and delivery standards, *marketing* solutions to problems, or *empowering* communities in a sense to take their fates into their own hands?

- Even if governments want to fully engage citizens, are citizens able and prepared to undertake these roles and responsibilities? Can they exercise a greater stake in decision-making? And how do we address the 'silent majority', how do we avoid capturing the views of the usual 'strong voices' and how do we look to future needs (the latent voices of the citizens of tomorrow)?

- Engagement can be costly; government is not a bottomless pit of resources to be expended in addressing whatever problems present themselves. How do we balance the desire for more personalised, tailored services against relentless demands for greater cost efficiency?

- Governments may not have the right skills, or be good at delivering services. Is it possible, then, that governments should *not* take on some community 'problems' but instead find ways to enable others to address them, facilitate community activism, reward initiatives and incentivise others with community and social goals.

Our contributors have grappled with these dilemmas and challenges, and with many more operational issues. Their job is to provide insight, open debate and awaken our sensibilities.

This volume is of particular relevance to public servants and others involved in policy design, implementation and delivery. For them we have brought together central players, agency deliverers, multiple jurisdictions, third sector providers, and the community of volunteers and public-spirited providers of community assistance.

ANZSOG is thrilled to be offering another challenging volume of essays; we trust you will come away with an abundance of valuable insights with immediate real-world applications. I would like to thank ANU E Press for its continued support over the ANZSOG publication series, and Justin Pritchard for assistance with the preparation of the final manuscript.

Allan Fels
Dean of ANZSOG
Sydney
April 2013

Contributors

John Alford is Professor of Public Sector Management at the Australia and New Zealand School of Government (ANZSOG) and at the Melbourne Business School (MBS), University of Melbourne, from which he is on extended secondment. He joined the MBS as a lecturer in 1988; before that he had been a manager in the Victorian Government responsible for industrial relations policy and change management, and lectured at RMIT. In 1982 he was a member of the Ministry of Transport Project Team which restructured the state's transport authorities, and in 1990 a member of the panel appointed by the premier to conduct a review of public service personnel management. His research, appearing in a variety of international journals, focuses on strategic management in the public sector, contracting and partnering, tackling 'wicked problems', and client-organisation relationships.

Rolf Alter is Director of Public Governance and Territorial Development at the Organisation for Economic Co-operation and Development (OECD), a post he has held since 2009. A German national, he joined the OECD in 1991, serving since 2006 as chief of staff of Secretary-General Angel Gurría. Prior to that, he was deputy director for public governance and territorial development and had worked in various other policy areas of the OECD. Prior to joining the OECD, Dr Alter was an economist in the Research Department of the International Monetary Fund (IMF), in Washington DC, and later moved to the IMF's African Department. He started his professional career in the German ministry of economy. Alter holds a doctorate from the University of Gottingen, Germany, following postgraduate work in Germany and the United States.

Ang Bee Lian was appointed Chief Executive Officer of Singapore's National Council of Social Service (NCSS) in 2007. She is a trained social worker with a Bachelor of Arts from the National University of Singapore (Department of Social Work and Psychology), and holds a Master of Science in social policy and planning from the London School of Economics. She has 30 years of experience in Singapore's Ministry of Community Development, Youth and Sports (MCYS), where she has worked on developing policies and implementing programs in the social service sector. She has held senior management appointments in MCYS for over 15 years. In 2000 Ms Ang was awarded the Outstanding Social Worker Award and in 2002 the Public Administration Medal (Silver).

Christian Bason has been Director of *MindLab* Denmark since 2007. Prior to joining *MindLab*, he specialised in public organisation and management practice in Ramboll Management, a consultancy firm. He is passionate about bettering the public sector's ability to meet the needs of citizens and society. Mr Bason is also a university lecturer, and has presented to and advised governments around the world. He is a regular columnist and blogger and the author of four books on leadership, innovation and change in the public sector, most recently *Leading Public Sector Innovation: Co-creating for a better society* (Policy Press, 2010). Mr Bason holds an MSc in political science from Aarhus University, executive education from Harvard Business School and the Wharton School, and is currently writing a PhD thesis on public managers as designers.

Yehudi Blacher is the former Secretary of the Victorian Department of Planning and Community Development and is a professorial fellow with the Centre for Public Policy, University of Melbourne. Mr Blacher was appointed as the first Secretary of the newly established Department for Victorian Communities (renamed the Department of Planning and Community Development in 2007) in December 2002. In this capacity he was responsible for 15 business units with approximately 600 staff and a budget of $800 million, providing advice to eight ministers on a wide range of areas. Prior to this appointment, he was deputy secretary of the Victorian Department of Premier and Cabinet and, before that, director of youth and family service in the Department of Human Services, Victoria. From 1991 until to 1996 he was the Victorian director of local government, responsible for overseeing major reforms of the Victorian system of local government.

Lynelle Briggs enjoyed an illustrious three-decade career in the Australian Public Service (APS). During this time she worked for the former Department of Social Security, the Department of the Prime Minister and Cabinet, the Department of Treasury and the then Department of Health and Aged Care. In November 2004 she was appointed APS Commissioner, a position to which she was re-appointed in 2007. In August 2007 Ms Briggs became the Chief Executive Officer of Medicare Australia, retiring from this post in July 2011. She is currently chairing a major inquiry into ACT health and safety laws in the Territory's construction industry.

Shane Chisholm is the Territorial Public Relations Director of the Salvation Army, New Zealand. Until June 2012 he was the manager of business engagement and integration at Housing New Zealand and, before that, the organisation's national customer services manager. At Housing NZ he was responsible for the development of a national strategy and associated program of work to enhance the corporation's customer service experience.

Mark Chmielewski is Manager of the Indigenous Management Support program within the Department of Agriculture and Food, Western Australia. He began work at the WA Department of Agriculture in 1999 as an agronomist in the state's wheat belt region, after graduating from Curtin University, Perth, where he studied plant pathology. Mr Chmielewski worked as a policy officer with the WA Minister for Agriculture from 2002 to 2005. In 2005, he began working with Aboriginal landholders (pastoralists and farmers) to establish the now highly successful Indigenous Landholder Service (ILS) program, operated by the department in partnership with the Indigenous Land Corporation. The ILS program provides support to over 70 Indigenous agricultural businesses throughout the state, covering an area of 5.5 million hectares.

Mary Craig is the Deputy Commissioner responsible for Corporate Services within Inland Revenue in New Zealand. Her extensive and varied career with Inland Revenue began in the early 1990s. Prior to assuming her current role, Ms Craig held several senior roles in the department, including as Acting Deputy Commissioner for business development and systems; group manager for the Office of the Chief Tax Counsel; national manager, business management services; senior advisor in child support and operational management positions in Manukau, Dunedin and Invercargill. She has a masters degree in business administration.

Adrienne Gillam is the South Australian Manager of the Regional Operations Centre and the Anangu Pitjantjatjara Yankuntjatjara (APY) Regional Office in Indigenous Housing, located in the Commonwealth Department of Families, Housing, Community Services and Indigenous Affairs. A career public servant, Adrienne Gillam began her working life in the Australian Public Service in 1984 with the then Commonwealth Employment Service and has worked in areas of service delivery since that time. She is passionate about delivering the Remote Service Delivery National Partnership (2009-14) under the government's 'Closing the Gap' initiative.

Michael Hansen is the Principal of Cairns West State School, Queensland, a low socio-economic partnership school enrolling a high percentage of Indigenous students. Under his leadership the main focus of the school has been engaging parents and the community to develop real partnerships over educational performance involving case management of all the students. Prior to this appointment he was an educational administrator with the Western Cape College at Weipa, Queensland and then Principal at Doomadgee State School, Queensland, where he took the lead role in establishing a Local Indigenous Partnership Agreement with the Doomadgee community.

Peter Houghton is the Manager of the State Reserve Strategy, a division of the New South Wales Land and Property Management Authority. His recent responsibilities have included the administration of over 260 caravan parks and camping grounds on Crown land, with which he assisted in business development planning and compliance issues, and chairing the Crown Lands Reserve Trust Management Steering Committee which oversaw reform in the management of some 900 community trust boards. He is on the State Parks

Trusts Advisory Board and is currently co-producing service outcomes with local communities through the preparation of plans of management for public recreation reserves.

Bette-Jo Hughes is Assistant Deputy Minister, Service BC, Province of British Colombia, Canada. Service BC provides service delivery to citizens and businesses through multiple access points including over the counter, telephone and online as well as registry services for citizens and the business community. Previously, Ms Hughes was the Executive Director of Service Delivery Operations and responsible for Service BC centres throughout the province. She has been involved in the development of service delivery agreements with the private sector, including the negotiation of the Service BC–IBM Alternative Service Delivery Agreement for the provision of web channel and contact centre services, and more recently with the Negotiated Request for Proposal for the Distribution of Liquor Project.

Gail Kelly is the National Manager of Research and head of the Research Corporate Strategy division in Inland Revenue, New Zealand, a position she has held since 2008. Leading a multi-disciplinary team, she provides input and strategic insights for most business areas across the Inland Revenue department and in relation to a number of important social support programs. Prior to that she worked in Australia's CSIRO and the Department of Agriculture, Fishery and Forests.

Don Kettl is Dean, School of Public Policy, University of Maryland and a non-resident Senior Fellow at the Brookings Institution. Prior to his appointment, he was the Robert A. Fox Leadership Professor at the University of Pennsylvania and Professor of Political Science. Dr Kettl is a student of public policy and public management and specialises in the management of public organisations. He is the author or editor of a dozen books and monographs, including: *The Next Government of the United States: why our institutions fail us and how to fix yhem*; *On Risk and Disaster: Lessons from Hurricane Katrina*; *The Global Public Management Revolution*; and, *Leadership at the Fed*. He is a fellow of Phi Beta Kappa and the National Academy of Public Administration.

Evert Lindquist is Professor and Director in the School of Public Administration at the University of Victoria, British Columbia, Canada. He served as Director from 1998–2009 before taking a two-year research sabbatical in 2010 and 2011, during which time he held the ANZSOG–ANU Chair in Applied Public Management Research at The Australian National University. Prof Lindquist resumed his post as Director in January 2012. He is also the editor of *Canadian Public Administration*, the journal of the Institute of Public Administration of Canada. He has published widely on public administration with his main areas of interest including: central decision-making, public sector reform, how governments address complex policy challenges, the role of think tanks and experts in the policy process, and exploring the potential of visualisation techniques for policy development.

Ian Mackie leads the Division of Indigenous Education and Training Futures in the Queensland Department of Education and Training. The division's goal is to improve outcomes for Indigenous students across the state. Mr Mackie's diverse career has included stints as a science and mathematics teacher, as an associate administrator and school principal, and as director of the Western Cape College, Weipa, Queensland. He has worked as the principal policy advisor on Indigenous education for the Education Department and as Executive Director of Community Engagement in the Queensland Department of the Premier and Cabinet. He was also the inaugural Training Ombudsman in Queensland. In 2012 Mackie was nominated for the Australian Government Minister's Award for Excellence in Teaching or Leadership in Aboriginal and Torres Strait Islander Education.

James Mowat is the Manager of the Regulatory Frameworks and Processes division in Land Information New Zealand (LINZ). He leads a team of regulatory specialists who support the work of LINZ regulators in the area of land titles, cadastral surveying, rating valuation and Crown land. LINZ follows an optimal regulation maxim of 'as little as possible, as much as necessary'. Mr Mowat has overseen a program transforming all of LINZ's regulatory rules, standards and guidelines, using international best practice with high levels of stakeholder engagement.

Jenny Pequignot is the Director of Natural Resource Programs in the Victorian Department of Sustainability and Environment, which invest in the health, resilience and biodiversity of Victoria's regional water catchment areas. Her expertise includes climate change, fisheries management, port administration and transport reform, and risk management. A graduate of ANZSOG's executive master's program, she has also served as the Executive Director in Forests and Parks, Victoria.

Nicole Pietrucha is Manager of Medicare Australia's Community Engagement Branch, a position she has held since July 2010. In this role she is responsible for Medicare's Stakeholder Engagement Team as well as its Co-design and Business Process teams. Integrating these three teams reflects a new approach to engagement management in Medicare. Her branch is charged with improving the organisation's relations with stakeholders and the community, as part of the 'service delivery reform agenda' adopted by the Commonwealth Department of Human Services, a process which begun in July 2011.

Fiona Rafter is Acting Assistant Director General of the Queensland Department of Community Safety, where she among other responsibilities oversees volunteer programs to assist in natural emergencies. She has previously been executive director in the Queensland Ministerial, Information and Legal Services Branch and worked at the Queensland Department of Corrective Services.

Jo Sammut is the Senior Project Manager for Service Delivery Integration in the South West Sydney Metropolitan Region, in the NSW Department of Family and Community Services. As community regeneration manager from 2006 to 2010, he led the development and implementation of Building Stronger Communities in Macquarie Fields, south-west Sydney, a $66 million place-based partnership initiative funded by Housing NSW to improve social and urban environments, support learning and employment, and improve service access in seven priority locations covering 22 disadvantaged social housing estates.

Jim Scully is the Principal of *ThinkPlace*, New Zealand. He has worked as a leader in large multi-nationals, government agencies and small businesses across the Asia-Pacific region. He has been involved in product and service development across these multiple sectors for 28 years. Previously, as a senior executive in Inland Revenue New Zealand, he introduced user-centred design and project management as professional capabilities. During this time he led a number of cross-agency and international initiatives, gaining valuable experience in the dynamics of co-creation across silos. His group was recognised in *Business Week* in an article titled 'What Obama needs to know about Innovation'.

Martin Stewart-Weeks is a Director in the Global Public Sector practice of the Cisco Internet Business Solutions Group (IBSG). He has more than 20 years experience in organisational management and consulting in the corporate and public sectors, working with ministers and officials and with a wide range of not-for-profit organisations. At Cisco his focus is primarily on developing Internet business solutions and online strategies for public sector organisations. He has held senior policy and advisory positions with both federal and state governments in Australia. His main interests are strategy, policy analysis, facilitation, and market and social research.

Gerry Stoker is Professor of Politics and Governance, School of Social Sciences, University of Southampton and Director of the Centre for Citizenship, Globalisation and Governance. Previously, Professor Stoker was the founding chair of the New Local Government Network acting as advisor to the UK government and the Council of Europe on local government issues for more than a decade. He has written extensively on local and regional government – their strategic directions, management, financing and organisation. He has written more than 20 authored or edited books and over 80 refereed articles or book chapters. *Why Politics Matters*, won the 2006 political book of the year award from the UK Political Studies Association. His research interests deal with issues of governance in complex settings, political disenchantment in Western democracies, citizen empowerment and strategies for encouraging civic behavior among citizens.

David Sweeney is the Director of Co-design Practice in the Commonwealth Department of Human Services, where he is responsible for redesigning 'customer journey experiences' for the disadvantaged members of the community, such as the unemployed and homeless. He has previously worked with the Australian Public Service Commission, and the National School of Government in the United Kingdom.

Deb Symons is an Associate at Cube Management Solutions, a Melbourne-based consultancy which aims to help the Victorian public sector provide services for the community. Her professional background lies in the emergency services sector, having been previously Assistant Director in the Victoria Police, the Manager of Business Solutions in the Country Fire Authority, and Executive Advisor to the chair of the Victorian Bushfire Reconstruction and Recovery Authority. Her experience spans organisational change, strategic and business planning, business case development and project planning, and service delivery across a broad range of areas including business services, information technology, and community development.

1. Putting Citizens First: Engagement in policy and service delivery for the 21st century

Evert Lindquist

During the late 2000s the theme of 'citizen-oriented government' steadily rose to the top of the public management agenda (OECD 2009). Governments at all levels have declared their interest in finding better ways to respond to and serve citizens and communities through better-designed programs and consultative processes (Advisory Group on the Reform of Australian Government Administration 2010; Bourgon 2011). For many, the theme of 'putting citizens first' is a natural extension of the new public management (NPM) initiatives, which sought to better serve citizens as clients and customers, leading to experimentation and institutionalisation of integrated service delivery and innovations such as Centrelink in Australia, Service Canada (Halligan and Wells 2008; Dutil et al. 2010) and the Common Measurement Tool in Canada, and New Zealand's Kiwi Counts. For others there are resonances with whole-of-government, joined-up government, and horizontal governance themes (Management Advisory Committee 2004), motivated by outside-looking-in perspectives.

Many observers point out that democratic governance has always been about better serving and engaging citizens, and that institutional reforms, which are informed by the advent of new technologies, can be traced back a hundred years and more. Despite the considerable experimentation and progress made by many governments over the last decade, the expectations about better connecting governments to citizens have increased. Elected leaders and officials are keen to lessen the distrust of citizens in government and build constructive support through better policy and higher quality services. Governments at all levels in Australia and New Zealand have been taking greater interest in measuring citizen satisfaction, and finding ways to work with citizens and communities to design services. Moreover, citizens and governments continue to see new possibilities in web-based technologies deriving from private sector innovation, and governments are under pressure to increase the value-for-money obtained from programs in increasingly tight fiscal environments. Most recently, the ambition of inculcating a citizen orientation when delivering services and designing policy animated Western Australia's Economic Audit Committee's *Putting the Public First: Partnering with the community and business to deliver outcomes* (October 2009) and the Commonwealth's *Ahead of the Game: Blueprint for the reform of Australian Government administration* (March 2010).

The themes of 'citizen-centred' or 'citizen-focused' government and governance have ever greater resonance because of the expanding opportunities presented by digital information and communications technology (ICT) (Borins et al. 2007; Roy 2008). It is now conceivable to think not only of citizen-*oriented* service and improved policy delivery, but genuinely citizen-*informed* and even citizen-*designed* and often specifically tailored interventions that are designed to accommodate the needs of individuals and communities — what some refer to as the 'individualisation' of policy and service delivery (Howard 2010). Such developments are consistent with the 'public value' perspective which calls on political leaders and public sector executives to explore myriad ways to provide services for citizens and communities (Moore 1995; Alford and O'Flynn 2009, 2012). Advocates for Government 2.0 and Open Government suggest that ICTs might drive governments to dramatically re-conceive the role of the public bureaucracies in delivering programs and designing policy (Dunleavy et al 2006; Government 2.0 Task Force 2009). Still others have referred to this as the 'service state' (Dutil et al. 2010; Wanna et al. 2010).

The theme of the Australia and New Zealand School of Government's (ANZSOG) 2011 annual conference in Sydney, 'Putting Citizens First' was designed to explore these ideas. Early in the planning process, the program committee[1] recognised that the phrase 'citizen-oriented' government or governance can mean different things to different people, and even committed practitioners and scholars can talk past each other when discussing how to better design, serve and work with citizens. Accordingly the conference was organized around four broad areas:

- *Integrating services for citizens*: searching for better ways to integrate the services that governments provide with the specific needs of different categories of citizens, clients or customers in mind, and offering readily accessible information on those services.

- *Discovering citizen needs and preferences*: systematically learning more about the experience of citizens in receiving the services delivered to them, and using that feedback to improve the delivery of those programs.

- *Engaging citizens in policy and service design*: improving how governments engage citizens in the design of policy and service delivery regimes, sometimes involving co-design and co-re-design of services and programs, and sometimes co-production.

---

1 The author sat on the 2011 ANZSOG annual conference steering committee. Beyond developing the program, however, it was the rest of the committee — Tracey Fisher, Peter Allen, Glen Sheldon, John Wanna, and many others — who did the heavy lifting in identifying and contacting speakers, organising logistics, and making the conference run smoothly. Sam Vincent did yeoman's work with speakers to develop the papers and reflections comprising this volume.

- *Improving public sector capability*: developing strategies to improve capacity and capabilities in government in order to make progress on all three of the above fronts.

These areas are distinct but often overlap. All have been energised by the possibilities afforded by tested and emerging ICTs.

The general goal of the conference was to take stock of the state of practice and recent innovation in serving and engaging citizens at the local, state and national levels in Australia and New Zealand. This progress was to be put in context by getting a sense of international practice and contemporary academic perspectives on citizen service delivery and engagement. Speakers were asked to share their experiences, and identify barriers and issues as well as practical, effective and value-added strategies for moving toward citizen-oriented government. Speakers and conference participants were asked to identify areas where governments and officials might better serve citizens with breakthrough reforms, particularly taking advantage of new technology.

While the conference themes — service integration, eliciting citizen feedback, engagement, and capacity — were not new, we identified several broad questions to ask of presenters about the state of the art, where governments had made the most progress, and where the potential was for making further progress:

- How much progress had governments made with respect to promoting integrated service delivery, working within and across governments, and what are the prospects for doing even more?
- How much progress had governments made with respect to obtaining citizen feedback on services they deliver, and are they making second-generation efforts to discovering citizen needs and preferences?
- How much progress had governments made with respect to engaging citizens and communities in service delivery and policy design matters, and can governments go further with respect to co-designing and co-delivering services?
- What needs to be done to build the culture, repertoires, and sensibilities in public sector organisations to respond to and anticipate demands for better services and engagement, and take advantage of technological possibilities which promise to put citizens first?

We invited keynote speakers who could offer conceptual but grounded perspectives on these questions as well as an impressive number of practitioners who could share recent experience on implementing citizen-oriented service delivery, measurement, and engagement strategies.

Several questions arise because of inherent tensions in our governance systems and different ideas of how to respond to citizen needs and interests. These include:

- Are Westminster governance systems, with their vertical accountabilities and divided responsibilities, necessarily incongruent with a citizen orientation, or can they be made to move faster and further?

- Can governments increase the trust of citizens in government by improving services and better engaging them, or will citizens continue to disengage from government no matter how much progress is made?

- How can citizen input be meshed with the input that inevitably comes from experts, stakeholders, and government agencies (often other levels of government)?

- Do governments provide what citizens and communities want or need, or do they focus on better providing services that governments have identified in certain ways?

- Is co-production the same thing as engaging citizens and deliberative democracy? If not, how does it differ, and how and when can they complement each other?

None of these tensions are new or deal-breakers for making headway. Indeed, the goal of the conference was to recognise and assess new possibilities for making progress: there are new technologies, two new generations of public servants and citizens taking on leadership roles as the post-World War II baby-boomers exit the stage, and no shortage of recent innovations to serve as exemplars and encouragement. This is a critical time to consider how to build capacity and make strategic investments focused on better working with and responding to citizens.

The conference was a success with 450 participants and 32 speakers, who were invited from Australia, New Zealand, Canada, Singapore, the United Kingdom, and the United States to provide diverse perspectives from different levels of government and sectors on strategies and experiences for putting citizens first. We designed the workshop sessions so that panellists spoke briefly to their cases studies of innovation in order to elicit dialogue with the audience about their own experiences.

This collection of essays, based on the presentations made at the conference, seeks to capture many of these insights.[2] The papers generally track the flow of the conference, although some have been re-grouped with others that cover similar ground. This volume is organised into five parts:

---

2   For another set of reflections, see Andrew Podger (2012).

Setting the Scene: The evolving landscape for citizen engagement

Drivers for Change: Innovations in citizen-centric governance

Case Studies: Land management and Indigenous empowerment

Case Studies: Fostering community engagement and connectedness

Case Studies: Engaging with information technology and new media

This chapter provides an overview of the themes and arguments of the volume and, in a sixth section, provides an assessment of where progress has been made in the citizen-oriented governance agenda, and identifies avenues for further dialogue and research.

1. Setting the scene: The evolving landscape for citizen engagement

Before delving into the drivers and approaches for canvassing and engaging citizens, the steering committee sought to provide perspective on the context in which putting citizens has been proceeding. We felt this was necessary because, as indeed many speakers noted, many of the motivations and aspiration behind more citizen-centred governance and government are not new — arguably, strands of these ideas have been at play for close to two decades. Even if progress has been made, and new possibilities are at hand, the strong interest in developing more of a citizen orientation connotes some impatience and urgency, implying inertia and possibly government resistance to these ideas. If the initiatives represented in this volume constitute the next wave of reform, do realistic strategies and expectations exist for dealing with the broader dynamics and tensions for better engaging and responding to citizens? Three speakers from outside Australia and New Zealand were invited to provide international and theoretical perspectives on these issues.

The conference began with a provocative question: can Westminster practice and reflexes, and the agendas of duly-elected governments, co-exist with efforts to improve service delivery and engage citizens or are they in considerable tension, as argued by Jeffrey Roy (2008)? In Chapter 2, Gerry Stoker argues that a more fundamental normative tension is at play about engaging citizens in Westminster and other systems: he contrasts an elite, party-driven 'protective approach' limiting government engagement to a 'developmental approach' which sees democracy and participation as fundamental values, leading to greater commitment to citizen engagement. Each, he argues, has their own weakness: the protective model resists change, the developmental model risks utopianism. Both proceed against a general climate of 'anti-politics' and lack of trust in governments and democracy in OECD countries, which leads to disengagement, blended with media saturation, high expectations of government, and the decline of traditional parties. Nevertheless, Stoker sees great potential to increase engagement, but governments must recognise citizens and communities have differing intensities of preference for engagement, and this requires understanding the motivators and inhibitors to engagement. He outlines a framework for systematically building capacity, involving citizens and groups as part of a broader civic infrastructure and multiple instruments which can be deployed depending on the type of citizen and community, and through 'nudges' (Stoker, 2011). Stoker suggests that, while governments need to take democracy seriously, they should resist catering to populist impulses, and manage expectations about the value that citizen engagement can add to policy and service design.

The possibilities for better engaging citizens has generated interest by governments around the world, which are simultaneously struggling with the implications for governing. Don Kettl took on the question 'Facilitating choice, letting go: are governments really willing to let citizens and communities determine policy choices and service mixes?' In Chapter 3, Kettl provides an interesting historical view rooted in recent US experience, but, like Stoker, also sees more fundamental forces at play. He depicts the NPM wave of reforms in the United States during the 1990s and beyond as essentially about better engaging and responding to citizens, along with being more efficient and accountable. He suggests that this wave of reform is a spent force in the United States, not to be succeeded by promising debates over the possibilities of co-production and responsive service delivery for citizens, but rather, by an uneasy and far more fundamental debate about the role of government in a resource-strapped environment. While considerable devolution and deregulation has occurred, he points to inconsistent public expectations of government. Even his more optimistic wonderment about the possibilities flowing from the open data movement to respond to citizen and community needs (Rat Rub-out Baltimore),[3] to show where services are distributed across the United States at different levels of aggregation, or to put community interventions and accountability on a different and more comprehensive footing, is chastened. He worries that citizens and communities simply might not care or be interested as they seek ever lower taxes and distrust government. Like Stoker, Kettl believes it will be important for governments to work hard to show that it is listening (and responding) to citizen needs.

---

3   Adam Bednar, 'Charles Village Rat Rub-out Produces Results', *North Baltimore Patch* (September 28, 2011) at http://northbaltimore.patch.com/articles/charles-village-rat-rub-out-produces-results

Animating government investments in improving service delivery was a hope that better service might lead to increased citizen trust in government (e.g., Heintzman & Marson 2005; Halligan & Wells 2008), but, as Stoker and Kettl note, citizens seem even more disconnected from their governments. Even if governments continue to make progress with citizen-oriented service delivery and engagement, will trust and satisfaction in government rebound, or will the gap continue to widen? In his keynote address, Rolf Alter of the Organisation for Economic Co-operation and Developments (OECD) addressed the topic of 'Citizens and governments: are they more connected or more disconnected?' In Chapter 4, Alter provides insights informed by several OECD studies and reports carried out over the last decade (OECD 2001, 2009 and 2011). He observes that during the 2000s, and since a succession of significant reports, the OECD has focused on citizens with respect to engaging on policy, open data and government. On the one hand, the interest of governments has emerged from genuine interest in citizen rights and expectations about engagement by their governments and the hope that more engagement might lead increased trust of government, but the real challenge for OECD leaders is how to engage in useful, productive, and cost-effective ways with sufficient information. Alter points out that exploring and taking advantage of the promise of social media and other digital technology will require new capacity and repertoires in government (see Chapter 9, this volume). He wonders whether the ability of citizens to organise and move faster than governments in response to political and other events through social media (some communities better than others), will outstrip government's other efforts to more evenly and systematically engage citizens, communities, and civil society organisations.

2. Drivers for change: Innovations in citizen-centric governance

Several speakers — internationally recognised innovators and thinkers in their respective areas — were invited to explore different approaches, techniques and frameworks for engaging citizens (Christian Bason, John Alford, Bette-Jo Hughes, Lynelle Briggs, and Martin Stewart-Weeks).[4]

Bason of Denmark's MindLab addressed the question of 'Engaging citizens on policy and service design: can this be meshed with input from experts, stakeholders and other governments?' Governments often engage citizens

---

4   The conference did not review the many different and emerging approaches for engaging citizens in consultation and deliberation. The focus was more on how diverse experts might assist in helping government to better understand citizen needs, as opposed to exploring how citizens, experts and stakeholders might better interact with each other in broader consultation and deliberative processes, and how governments can better balance these inputs.

and experts sequentially, but, in Chapter 5, Bason describes how they can be fused to more fully understand the experience of citizens and, in turn, design better policies and services that can lead to threshold increases in the quality of outcomes. He argues that significant rethinking of public services is required due to a 'perfect storm' of relentless change, the demographic rollover, the innovative nature and declining costs of technology, and the increasing expectations of citizens about the quality and fit of services. He describes how different research and design processes of MindLab are calibrated to understand challenges and incubate new ways to deliver services, all proceeding with the goal of 'co-creating' policy and public services with those who will use them. Bason reviewed examples of how MindLab staff ask or draw out individuals about their experiences in trying to access and use a service, and work with them to identify whether it could be delivered better — this means that members of the research team often need to put themselves in the shoes of clients and undertake systematic and creative enquiry to gain insight and to challenge assumptions (Bason 2010). This requires engaging citizens in new ways, using a variety of techniques (not just surveys, but qualitative information and other approaches such as film, ethnography, art, visual tools, role-playing and mapping). Bason and his colleagues seek to engage not only a wide circle of users but also a broad circle of experts and other professionals who look at problems differently. As we will see later, this engagement and design sensibility has informed recent practice in the Australian and New Zealand governments.

Alford offers a broad framework for understanding how public services are already co-produced with citizens and clients, an important perspective to have in mind before considering how to innovate. He tapped his award-winning research (Alford 2009) to address the topic of 'engaging citizens in co-producing service outcomes'. Alford's insight is that when considering how services are provided to citizens, whether directly by governments or other entities, citizens are usually involved in varying degrees in co-producing those services through diverse contributions (for example, by filling out forms or making requests), and this may be done for material or non-material reasons. Alford's perspective goes beyond the citizen and ostensible deliverer to encompass the whole chain of upstream and downstream contributors, who create conditions or enable services to occur. His argument is that, before considering designing policy or new services (what we could call co-creation or co-design), one should appreciate the extent of co-production already relied upon. In his view, co-creation and co-production should not be about getting citizens to shoulder more of the costs of service delivery, but rather to understand that co-production works under certain circumstances, with a mix of motivations and interdependency. As for Briggs (Chapter 6), he points out this mix and balance varies significantly across beneficiaries, obligators or regulators, and volunteers, depending on the service.

Engaging citizens in research and design is only the latest effort to better understand how citizens experience the delivery of services. Hughes from the British Columbia Public Service and representing Canada's Institute for Citizen-Centred Service Delivery, canvasses the evolution of efforts to obtain feedback from citizens and measure attributes of service delivery, which resulted in a collaborative cross-government centre-of-excellence. In Chapter 5, Hughes addresses the topic 'Measuring citizen feedback: what is citizen satisfaction? What is the state of the art?' She reviews the origins of the Citizens First movement, the interest in understanding the drivers of customer satisfaction with public services, the development of the Citizens First methodology and the Common Measurement Tool, and the establishment of the institute to further the idea of measuring the quality of service across governments within and across national boundaries (Dinsdale and Marson 1999; Schmidt & Strickland 1998a, 1998b; Marson & Heintzman 2009). Consistent with the themes of the Putting Citizens First conference, there has been growing interest by Canadian governments in complementing these measurement tools with qualitative approaches for involving citizens in a conversation about the kind and mix of services and policy they or their communities would like to receive (Howard 2010). Hughes also notes that the BC Government has recently announced its policy on open data and government, informed by the previous work of Australia and New Zealand governments.

In Chapter 6, Briggs shifts gears, moving from considering citizen engagement and the re-design of specific policy and services to merging and re-orienting bureaucracies in order to provide more integrated and better tailored services. As then head of Medicare Australia, Briggs was part of the leadership team merging three organisations — Medicare Australia, Centrelink, and Department of Human Services — to better integrate service delivery and policy interventions for health services, income support and child support. In her words the goal is to 'truly put people at the centre of everything we do'. This is a significant task involving structural, technological, and cultural change, involving a total of 40,000 staff, 550 offices, and 170 programs. Briggs describes how, along with new technology and diverse delivery channels, the emerging organisation is seeking to establish new ways of listening to and working with client, customer, citizen, and communities by means of community forums with staff and other techniques such as building citizen pathways (see Chapter 13) in order to better understand needs and tailor service mixes. Briggs observes that public agencies must be well organised, focused, and culturally disposed in order to properly engage citizens and their communities on an ongoing basis, which also requires sustained and visionary leadership.

Stewart-Weeks addresses the topic of 'Citizens, government and technology: what are the unrealised and emerging possibilities?' In Chapter 9, he briefly outlines how governments are starting to reshape conversations with citizens using social media, and how this process is not only growing, but, as Alter notes, is often driven from outside government, not from within it. Referring to Jocelyn Bourgon's New Synthesis project (Bourgon 2011), Stewart-Weeks notes that increased connectivity is not the same as greater connectedness and a culture of openness, sharing and co-creating. For government this implies 'having richer and more meaningful conversations with citizens who are increasingly learning to live in the world of pull and are increasingly frustrated by the world of push', where governments send information to be consumed by citizens rather than discussed. Stewart-Weeks identifies examples of government turning to Twitter, using videos to spark community dialogue, relying on Facebook as part of emergency responses, to elicit innovative ideas in concerted ways. He argues that private sector and public sector organisations are realising that citizens and external networks often know more than they do, and can respond faster. The trick is to recognise and embrace this dynamic, adopting new ways to monitor and tap that information and knowledge, and supplying data for citizen use in ways which might surprise government leaders, while not relinquishing 'old' means of engagement that are useful for certain purposes. Stewart-Weeks labels entities making this shift as 'edge organisations' with 'a fundamentally different power topology from traditional organisations', prepared to have 'bouncy' dialogues with citizens containing seeds for innovation and increased productivity. He argues making this shift will be essential in the future, where experimentation and emergence will become bigger facets of how governments, citizens and communities create public value.

Many of the themes explored in these presentations were taken up in the workshop sessions, which probed more specific cases. What follows provides summaries of these cases in three sections: land management and Indigenous empowerment; fostering community engagement and connectedness; and engaging with information technology and new media. Section 6 steps back to consider where progress has been made for putting citizens first, and where it has not, the implications for building capacity and strategic awareness in public service organisations, and issues which need to be taken up in further detail.

3. Case studies: Land management and Indigenous empowerment

This section introduces several cases on working with local organisations to manage land resources or increase the capacity of Indigenous communities, or both. We begin with three initiatives that rely on networks to deal with, respectively, remediating degraded farm land in Victoria, state reserves in New South Wales, and Indigenous landholders in the Kimberley, and then consider three diverse perspectives on empowering Indigenous communities.

Australia, of course, has vast territories which need to be managed and the issues that managing this land raises are often beyond the scope of traditional government service delivery. Three cases explore some interesting approaches:

- Jenny Pequignot (Chapter 10) describes how a coalition of farmers in north-western Victoria, collaboratively addressing land degradation issues, became a much larger network of entities now called Landcare. Initiated in the late 1980s, Landcare is now a collective of community-based and volunteer natural resource management groups. It relies on local citizens to tackle issues, lever other resources and networks, and requires limited government support. Pequignot observes that government representatives regularly engage and listen, essentially working as a junior partner in the relationship and resisting treating the network as a government delivery arm.

- Peter Houghton (Chapter 11) reviews how New South Wales manages its land reserves by means of community trust boards and volunteers. Houghton reviews how caravan park operators and the Crown Lands Division partnered to create the Caravan and Camping NSW website to improve quality and use of facilities, which is also a vehicle for accountability.

- Mark Chmielewski (Chapter 12) chronicles the origins of the Indigenous Landholders Service and the entrepreneurial leadership and dialogue with communities, along with collaborative and multi-faceted long-term solutions, that are now hallmarks of the service

Chapter 13 provides other perspectives exploring how to strengthen engagement and empower Indigenous Australians. Adrienne Gillam of the Department of Families, Housing, Community Services and Indigenous Affairs describes how, the impetus of the Remote Service Delivery National Partnership was dedicated to 'closing the gap' by introducing a different way of working with Indigenous communities. The second example in the chapter is a case explored by Ian Mackie of Queensland's Department of Education and Training. The department champions distinct, targeted and collaborative strategies for improving achievement in education achievement. His colleague, Michael Hansen, Principal of Cairns West State School, amplifies these points, observing that principals are critical because they can develop incentives, and work with parents and teachers, to improve student attendance and achievement.

4. Case studies: Fostering community engagement and connectedness

Although there can be no fast distinctions, the case studies in this section provide examples of social policy interventions relying on engagement with citizens, communities and networks to achieve goals and often tailored approaches. The cases have been arrayed to move from higher to lower levels of analysis: national, state, organisational, and on the ground.

Ang Bee Lian (Chapter 14) describes how Singapore's social safety net and human service provisions have promoted self-reliance, with family as the first line of support and considered the basic building block of society. She describes how the government has sought to more proactively work with a 'many helping hands' approach by developing partnerships among government agencies, private and community agencies, business and educational institutions, social-cultural and religious organisations in order to increase social inclusion and social capital, and often requiring experimentation and innovation.

Yehudi Blacher (Chapter 15), former chief executive for the Victorian Government, describes the 10-year process of merging planning and community development in the state of Victoria to develop stronger and more resilient communities. A key lesson here is that a broad goal of understanding the state of cohesion and services in communities across the state requires sustained and often creative effort, working within and across levels of government.

Shane Chisholm (Chapter 16) describes how Housing New Zealand (HNZC) has engaged in a multi-year, top-to-bottom organisational transformation process since 2009, which has focused on better serving customers. Chisholm notes that reporting and actively seeking data and feedback of all kinds met resistance early on, but has become more accepted and part of the organisational culture.

Chapter 17 provides three different examples of organisations seeking to improve how they secure customer feedback.

- James Mowat describes how Land Information New Zealand (LINZ) underwent a profound shift since 2004 to move from a statutory-driven to more a consultative, strategic and efficient approach with the regulated stakeholder community. This process was informed by internal reviews, stakeholder expert committees and other forms of feedback, as well as sustained executive leadership.
- Jim Scully of ThinkPlace NZ reviews the approach that his firm takes when working with clients seeking to engage citizens. Scully stresses the need to

understand customer pathways, both with respect to the trajectory of their own circumstances and obtaining services from client organizations.

- David Sweeny, Director of Co Design Practice with the Commonwealth Department of Human Services, has drawn on the MindLab approach to undertake exploratory research with client groups, and mapped and developed visualisations of the experiences they have, as part of a service delivery reform initiative (see Briggs, Chapter 7).

The two cases in Chapter 18 focus more directly on ways to engage citizens and communities:

- Nicole Pietrucha of Medicare Australia's Community Engagement Branch provides a community-level view of their re-design process and how to build co-design capability.
- Jo Sammut of the NSW Department of Family and Community Services describes how the Building Stronger Communities (BSC) initiative was implemented in the Sydney suburb of Macquarie Fields.

In Chapter 19, Deb Symons the former head of the Victorian Bushfire Recovery and Reconstruction Authority's community engagement team, provides insights into how her team worked with devastated communities to shape the rebuilding process. Symons notes that strong executive leadership backing is required for the approach that was taken by her team to succeed, and front-line managers and staff require excellent facilitation, negotiation, and arbitration skills.

5. Case studies: Engaging with information technology and new media

Several workshop sessions had case studies which focused on the use of new information and social media technologies in different contexts. These are presented here as a complement to the Rat Rub-out case mentioned by Kettl (Chapter 4) describing the tools used in very different contexts, the Queensland emergencies and consultation processes by the New Zealand Inland Tax Revenue for tax legislation.

In Chapter 20, Fiona Rafter of Queensland's Department of Community Safety, reminds us of the tremendous number of emergencies and disasters which wrecked havoc on Queensland during late 2010 and early 2011. Her paper observes that managing the contribution of volunteers requires investments of time, training, others cost, recognition, and people management and she points out that government leaders have to recognise how bureaucratic culture and incongruent recruitment and other policies might create barriers for recruiting and retaining volunteers.

Mary Craig, Deputy Commissioner of Inland Revenue New Zealand's Corporate Services, describes in Chapter 21 how her organisation has been experimenting with online forums to engage a wider range of citizens about tax policy than with traditional consultation processes. Craig concludes that this experience has caused IRNZ to look at consultation differently, take risks, and continue to explore how to use different media to engage with citizens. Chapter 22, by Gail Kelly of IRNZ's Research Corporate Strategy group provides more detail on the experimentation engaged in by the service.

6. Putting citizens first: What has been accomplished and learned?

An overarching goal of the 2011 ANZSOG conference was to take stock of progress towards integrated service delivery, measuring citizen satisfaction, and encouraging citizen engagement and co-production, and to identify where further progress could be made. Another goal was to ascertain what capabilities and capacities were needed inside government to continue making progress in the 'putting citizens first' agenda. This section addresses the questions animating the conference and also provides several insights about capability.

1. How much progress has been made on integrated service delivery, working within and across governments?

It is difficult to arrive at any other conclusion than governments are trying to make progress on integrated service delivery models, but this work proceeds at different levels of analysis. So, for example, not only has the Commonwealth Government continued with its Centrelink model, but it has expanded it to include Medicare Australia and the Department of Human Services. Such integration clearly involves backroom and front-room elements, with the latter certainly focused not simply on government-redesigned service delivery, but, more expansively, on including citizens and communities. Also represented are examples from New Zealand Housing Corporation which has been transforming its culture, systems, and repertoires for engagement around its customer promise. Undoubtedly there are more examples from different departments and agencies in Australia and New Zealand at the national, state, and local levels. It also seems clear that governments are proceeding with integration only with certain clusters of service that are delivered either by the same or cognate organisations associated with a given level of government.

There are examples of Commonwealth and state initiatives engaging communities along with other government, business and non-profit organisations to develop partnerships. If the cases at the conference are in anyway representative, however, integrated service-delivery initiatives tend to be driven by one level of government, and other organisations are likely to be invited to participate during the implementation phase.

In short, there has been far less progress working *across* levels of government to present an integrated face and experience to citizens. This may constitute the next generation of service-delivery for governments, once they are ready, or citizens demand that it start happening.

2. How much progress has been made in obtaining citizen feedback on services and shaping new citizen-oriented service mixes?

Many Australian and New Zealand departments and agencies are aware of the Citizens First initiative and the measurement tools developed by the Institute for Citizen Centred Service Delivery. New Zealand introduced its own variation on the Citizens First methodology with Kiwi Counts, and other agencies have adopted similar approaches to measuring feedback through surveys of citizens and clients. The Victorian Government has systematically required local communities to measure citizen satisfaction and preferences on a wide variety of services, thereby providing broader and more integrated perspectives on the health and connectedness of those communities. The key drivers for making sense of progress continue to be regular reporting and accountability.

One element of Cosmo Howard's (2010) critique of Citizens First-type methodology is that customer satisfaction surveys might only focus on services that governments had chosen to deliver, the manner in which they had chosen to deliver them, and using criteria and a measurement tool that, while informed by citizen surveys, might not reflect the questions and issues citizens might raise in the context of particular services. He calls for more engagement with citizens to learn about what mix and channels of service they would provide and, where possible, to ascertain if they could be tailored for the specific needs of citizens and communities. As this volume demonstrates, many governments and public service leaders have turned that corner, embracing a more fulsome mix of methods for securing feedback and advice from citizens and communities.

The audience greatly appreciated Bason's keynote address at the conference, but many departments and agencies in Australia and New Zealand were already familiar with and been inspired by MindLab's innovative approaches (Bason 2010). Much of the MindLab approach draws on the practice of architecture and urban planning firms of hosting 'charrettes' to intensively work on designs and prototypes with experts and stakeholders, but also folds in other means for understanding the lives and needs of citizens. Clearly, consulting practices like ThinkPlace NZ are starting to fill this niche in this hemisphere. Even when some of the cases examined in this volume did not specifically seek to rely on such techniques, extended engagement and dialogue were intended to develop a citizen-based view of needs, priorities, and service mixes. If governments did not have such capacity to undertake such work, they were contracting for it and, in some cases, steadily building internal capabilities in this regard.

3. How much progress has been made in engaging and co-designing with citizens and communities in service delivery and policy design matters?

The papers in this volume suggest that vanguard departments and agencies have been adopting new approaches to engaging citizens with respect to service delivery, and in some cases bringing a wider circle of internal and external experts into the conversation about needs and design. There are examples of specific agencies transforming themselves, or building new units and capabilities to engage and work with citizens and communities. In many cases, the process was about trust-building, the sharing of information, and developing shared views and representations of existing patterns in service delivery and, in a few cases, new directions and partnerships.

For many contributors, however, the ultimate goal would be to have governments co-designing policy and service delivery regimes with citizens. The evidence does not suggest that there has been any significant movement towards 'macro' co-design of policy and service-delivery regimes in Australia and New Zealand. Nor should we expect Westminster systems to easily make such a change; governments find it difficult to co-design with each other, let alone with citizens. That said, important innovations can emerge from more circumscribed co-design arrangements on a local or national level.

Government representatives at the Putting Citizens First conference appreciated that engaging citizens and communities can no longer simply be about surveys, customer feedback, or a few visits. Rather, to be effective, citizen engagement requires making strategic investments over time, choosing the right kind of representatives and support, and steadily building trust over long periods of time. It is serious business, which has to be undertaken well, and yet, despite the need to ensure regular reporting and indicators of progress for those involved, it is often difficult to definitively show the effectiveness of such initiatives with respect to more effective programs, efficiency or lower costs. More importantly, it is widely recognised that more systematically engaging citizens requires new capabilities and skills inside government, as well as new systems for obtaining and sharing information.

This latter point broaches the theme of 'open government', which is different from engagement as a co-creating activity and, rather, involves sharing data so that outsiders can create value in often surprising ways (e.g., Kettl's example of Baltimore's Rat Rub-out, Queensland's use of social media to deal with emergencies and volunteers, and New Zealand's use of Twitter and Facebook to inform citizens of tax consultations). Like social media more generally, leaders in government have to prepare bureaucracies to better anticipate, see possibilities, and develop a degree of comfort with how such data and technology can be used.

4. What capabilities need to be developed in government to better respond to and anticipate citizen demands for better services and engagement?

This volume offers insights about the capabilities required for dealing with citizens and communities, either directly or indirectly. What follows distils and clusters these observations under several themes:

Aligning government capabilities for a citizen focus

- Develop an internal vision and new staff mind-sets first.
- Find and assign committed and visionary leaders to accomplish goals.
- Don't rely solely on a few leaders: build teams and supporting capabilities.
- Build internal structures and systems first to support critical external tasks.
- Keep executives and ministers informed.
- Build collaborative capabilities and expertise with other organisations.

Developing new perspectives on possibilities

- Use diverse ways to build perspective and develop 'professional empathy'.
- Engage diverse citizen representatives and different kinds of experts; look broadly.
- Ensure that staff are familiar with citizen and community needs.
- Develop comprehensive perspectives on service chains and environments.
- Share findings and validate information.

Managing discovery, change and engagement processes

• Develop a long view on the engagement/change process.

• Identify multiple channels for feedback and engagement, including social media.

• Consult on how best to engage given citizen needs and preferences.

• Sustained listening is critical for problem-solving and delivery solutions.

• Seek feedback and data on the performance of your organisation.

• Genuine co-creation requires sharing decisions, not securing endorsement.

• Act like a 'junior partner' in networks and communities.

• Don't try to convert networks and partnerships into service arms.

• Be prepared to work and respond in new ways.

• Develop priorities, and focus energy in promising, fundamental areas.

• Removing impediments is as important as finding new ways to work.

• Don't promise what can't be delivered; follow through with commitments.

Reporting and accountability

• Build accountability into the engagement process.

• Regularly report on progress to stakeholders, executives, ministers.

• Identify different phases of transformation/engagement; consider exit plans.

This list is not meant to serve as a 'one-size-fits-all' checklist that should be applied in all efforts to engage, work with, and serve citizens and communities. But it does summarise a good deal of the wisdom that is contained in this collection, albeit from very diverse and specific cases. Parallel to Stoker's opening observations, it is important to have a broad perspective and repertoires on how to engage and serve citizens, and then to carefully identify the right mix for the tasks and circumstances at hand. Nor should the list be seen as more competencies to be piled onto those already expected of front-line staff, middle managers, and executives across government. Rather, it points to the qualities governments should seek in a critical subset of leaders and staff who can make big difference — with the right support — by influencing much larger groups of people inside and outside government when engaging citizens.

This latter point should mollify the concerns of some observers (see Podger 2012), who worry about whether the sensibility advocated by 'putting citizens first' could lead to excessive focus on responding to citizen needs and providing tailored service at the expense of government priorities and budget constraints in our Westminster system. While the vertical accountability structure and often closed decision-making processes associated with cabinet governance can hamper more aggressive efforts to engage and respond to citizens, and recognising that successive duly elected governments will have distinct priorities, the cases reviewed from Australia, New Zealand and other countries show that experimentation and progress on 'putting citizens first' can proceed in very different governance contexts.

Finally, while the list above points to building capability for specific initiatives independently in departments and agencies, capability should also be developed *across* departments and agencies, and even *across* governments. There are so many potential approaches for engaging with citizens and for better understanding their needs and those of communities, it may be difficult for even the biggest departments to keep up with emerging approaches. The recent announcement of the Centre for Excellence in Public Sector Design, an 18-month pilot funded by the Australian Public Service Secretaries Board for the Commonwealth government and located at The Australian National University, is a promising sign. A similar capability could be developed for different approaches to engaging citizens, since Australian and New Zealand universities are repositories of world-class expertise in this area.

References

Advisory Group on the Reform of Australian Government Administration. 2010. *Ahead of the Game: Blueprint for the reform of Australian Governmentadministration*. Canberra: Commonwealth of Australia.

Alford, J. 1998. 'A Public Management Road Less Travelled: Clients as co-producers of public services', *Australian Journal of Public Administration*, v. 57:4 (December), pp. 128–37.

———. 2009. *Engaging Public Sector Clients: From service-delivery to co-production*. Palgrave Macmillan.

Alford, J. and O'Flynn J. 2009. 'Making Sense of Public Value: Concepts, critiques and emergent meaning', *International Journal of Public Administration*, v. 32, pp. 171–91.

——— and ———. 2012. *Rethinking Public Service Delivery: Managing with external providers*. Palgrave.

Australia, Government 2.0 Task Force. 2009. Engage: Getting on with Government 2.0, Report of the Government 2.0 Task Force (22 December). Canberra: Commonwealth of Australia.

Bason, Christian. 2010. *Leading Public Sector Innovation: Co-creating for a better society*. Policy Press.

Bingham, L.B., Nabatchi, T. and O'Leary, R. 2005. 'The New Governance: Practices and processes for stakeholder and citizen participation in the work of government', *Public Administration Review*, v. 65:5 (September/October), pp. 547–58.

Borins, S., Kernaghan, K., Brown, D., Bontis, N., Perri 6 and Thompson, F., (eds). 2007. *The Digital State: At the leading edge*. Toronto: University of Toronto Press.

Bovaird, T. 2007. 'Beyond Engagement and Participation: User and community coproduction of public services', *Public Administration Review* (September/October), pp. 846–60.

Boyle, D., and Harris, M. 2009. *The Challenge of Co-production: How equal partnerships between professionals and the public are crucial to improving public services*, Discussion Paper (December). London: New Economics Foundation.

Christensen, T. and Laegreid, P., eds. 2002. *The New Public Management: The transformation of ideas and practice*. Burlington, Vermont: Ashgate.

—— and ——, eds. 2007. *Transcending New Public Management: The transformation of public sector reforms* (Burlington, Vermont: Ashgate, 2007).

Dinsdale, G. and Marson D.B. 1999. *Citizen/Client Surveys: Dispelling myths and redrawing maps*. Ottawa: Canadian Centre for Management Development. Available at www.csps-efpc.gc.ca/pbp/pub/pdfs/P90_e.pdf.

Dutil, P., Howard, C.. Langford, J. and Roy, J. 2010. *The Service State: Rhetoric, reality and promise*. University of Ottawa Press.

Dunleavy, P., Margetts, H., Bastow, S. and Tinkler, J. 2006. 'New Public Management is Dead: Long live digital-era governance', *Journal of PublicAdministration Research and Theory*, v. 16:3, pp. 467–94.

Economic Audit Committee. 2009. *Putting the Public First: Partnering with the community and business to deliver outcomes*. Perth: State of Western Australia.

Halligan, J. and Wells, J. 2008. *The Centrelink Experiment: Innovation in service delivery*. Canberra: ANU E Press. Available at: epress.anu.edu.au/anzsog/centrelink/pdf/prelims.pdf.

Heintzman, R. and Marson, B. 2005. 'People, Service and Trust: Is there a public sector value chain?', *International Review of Administrative Sciences*, v. 71:4, pp. 549–75.

Hendriks, Carolyn M. 2012. 'Participatory and collaborative governance', in Rodney Smith, Ariadne Vroman and Ian Cook (eds), *Contemporary Politics in Australia: Theories, practices and issues*. Cambridge University Press.

Howard, C. 2010. 'Are we being served? A critical perspective on Canada's Citizens First satisfaction surveys', *International Review of Administrative Sciences*, v 76:1, pp. 65–83.

John, P., Cotterill, S., Richardson, L., Moseley, A., Smith, G., Stoker, G. and Wales, C. 2011. *Nudge, Nudge, Think, Think: Using experiments to change civic behaviour*. London: Bloomsbury Academic.

Kernaghan, K. 2005. 'Moving Toward the Virtual State: Integrating services and service channels for citizen-centred service', *International Review of Administrative Sciences*, v. 71:1, pp. 119–31.

——. 2009. 'Moving Towards Integrated Public Governance: Improving service delivery through community engagement'. *International Review of Administrative Sciences*, v. 75:2, pp. 239–54.

Lindquist, E. 2010. 'From Rhetoric to Blueprint: The Moran Review as concerted, comprehensive and emergent strategy for public service reform', *Australian Journal of Public Administration*, v. 69:2 (June), pp. 115–51.

Marson, B. and Heintzman, R. 2009. *From Research to Results: A decade of results-based service improvement in Canada*. Toronto: Institute of Public Administration of Canada. Available at: www.ipac.ca/documents/NewHorizonsmarsonandheintzman.pdf.

Matheson, A. and Szwarc, D. 2008. *Public Sector Service Value Chain: Linking employee engagement and customer satisfaction*. Victoria: BC Stats. Available at: www.bcstats.gov.bc.ca/data/ssa/reports/WES/WES2008-EmployeeCustomerLink.pdf.

Moore, Mark H. 1995. *Creating Public Value: Strategic management in government*. Harvard University Press.

OECD. 2001. *Citizens as Partners: OECD handbook on information, consultation and public participation*. Paris.

——. 2009. *Focus on Citizens: Public engagement for better policy and services*. Paris.

——. 2011. *The Call for Innovative and Open Government: An overview of country initiatives*. Paris.

Podger, A. 2012. 'Putting Citizens First: A priority that needs to be addressed with care', *Australian Journal of Public Administration*, v. 71:1 (March), pp. 85–90.

Smith, G. 2005. *Beyond the Ballot: 57 democratic innovations from around the world*. London: The Power Inquiry.

Schmidt, F. and Strickland, T. 1998a. *Client Satisfaction Surveying: Common Measurements Tool*. Ottawa: Canadian Centre for Management Development. Available at www.gov.mb.ca/stem/stm/pdfs/CCSN_CMT.pdf.

—— and ——. 1998b. *Client Satisfaction Surveying: A manager's guide*. Ottawa: Canadian Centre for Management Development. Available at www.gov. mb.ca/stem/stm/pdfs/CCSN_CMT.pdf.

Roy, J. 2008. 'Beyond Westminster Governance: Bringing politics and public service into the networked era', *Canadian Public Administration*, v. 51:4 (December), pp. 541–68.

Wanna, J., Butcher, J. and Freyens, B. 2010. *Policy in Action: The challenge of service delivery*. Sydney: University of New South Wales Press.

Part I. Setting the Scene: The evolving landscape for citizen engagement

2. Engaging Citizens: Can Westminster coexist with meaningful citizen-centric engagement?

Gerry Stoker

In this chapter I want to explore six topics. First, to recognise that with much of the discussion concerning 'putting citizens first' and embracing more meaningful forms of democracy, there is an inherent normative and developmental dimension. For me, the topic of citizen engagement is framed in the context of a significant scale of 'anti-politics' in the popular culture of many countries. Turning to solutions to this issue, I next argue the need to recognise that there is no such thing as an 'average citizen', and that we need to develop audits and tools that are capable of embracing the full diversity of communities. I will argue, furthermore, that because of the necessity of blending different factors, designing the right solution is likely to be a matter of judgment. Finally, I end with a plea to take democracy seriously.

Competing definitions of democracy

First, to deal with the notion of democracy. There are many ways to characterise the different models of democracy, but a broad distinction that David Held has put forward in his book *Models of Democracy* (1987) is between those that offer a protective framing of the issues of democracy and those that offer a developmental framing.

The protective model of democracy can be explained simply as a competition between elected leaders involving organised group engagement; and that understanding of democracy is, in part, built out of a fear of the problems associated with over-engaging with citizens. According to this definition, traditionally, it was necessary to construct a form of democracy that, in effect, held back mass citizen engagement, but gave people enough engagement and enough participation to feel that they were able to influence the system. The goals of this form of democracy were to protect liberties (both of property and of human rights), and to construct stable government.

Developmental framing is the other traditional way of characterising democracy. It expresses democracy as a fundamental human right; that individuals have the right to have a say over the things that affect them. Citizen engagement is central to this understanding of democracy because, so the argument goes, it builds better human beings and a better society. The goals of this second model are to create legitimate and effective outcomes, but stemming from shared learning and exchange of interests and ideas. Through sharing their understanding of problems and potential solutions, the fullest expression of citizenship in such a democracy is realised.

As these are two fundamentally different models, one should not assume that the arguments made in this volume of essays are normative-free. This is a normative-influenced zone and in effect, one can see the tension immediately in the title of my contribution, because Westminster and the Westminster model of governance is more in tune with the protective model of democracy than citizen-centric engagement, which is more compatible, by contrast, to the developmental model of democracy.

So, central to the themes discussed in this volume is a fundamental shift, as it were, from one understanding of democracy to another. For this reason these issues are often difficult to resolve because, in effect, much of what we as practitioners in and scholars of this field have been trying to do over the last two or three decades is graft the developmental model of democracy on to a protective model of democracy. This has resulted in a degree of confusion and tension.

These tensions, then, find expression in the debate concerning the prioritisation of representative forms of democracy in favour of direct or participative forms of democracy; whether we recognise the impact and importance of the development of critical and challenging citizens.

When it comes to the topic of citizen engagement with government, if we compare the 1950s with the present, there is evidence in nearly all Organisation for Economic Co-operation and Development (OECD) countries of a rise in the number of critical and challenging citizens, and that more citizens are interested in politics than they were four or five decades ago.

Furthermore, over this period, citizens' engagement and their involvement in politics has become less formal. It is conducted less through conventional institutions (for example, political parties) than through involvement in 'single issue' politics and, more generally, through civil society, social media and the Internet. At the same time, however, politics itself has become more centralised. There is now a focus on leaders instead of their parties, a trend that has come to define the modern political era. Running concurrent to this are constitutional trends, which have encouraged pluralism and devolution. There is also an increasing focus on the professionalisation of politics, meaning many politicians do not have any other professional experience to draw upon from their working life. And yet, there is a growing call in many countries for political systems to better reflect the diversity of the societies they represent.

These changes have come amidst the backdrop of the modern 24-hour news cycle with its emphasis on 'sound byte democracy' and the rise of civic journalism's use of the Internet as a way of projecting alternative news arguments and news agendas. Having briefly mentioned some of these political developments of the past 50 years, it is clear that the era has been one of contradictions and challenges.

Democracy and the changing face of citizen–government engagement

So, how are these two models of democracy responding to these trends? As far as the Westminster model is concerned, there is a degree of nervousness about increasing citizen engagement. This is because, from a protective perspective, it would be understandable to be cautious and concerned about how far citizens can push the state. Undoubtedly the Westminster model is feeling the pressure from increased citizen engagement, reflected in the increasing demands and challenges that originate with the citizens themselves.

Turning to the developmental model, there are some positive and reform-minded trends that should be discussed. There are also some positive examples of change, but there is also the spectre of utopianism: designing forms of participation and engagement that are not compatible with the way people actually live their lives.

In terms of being equipped to function within the contemporary milieu of a stubborn anti-politics, both democratic models need to go through a period of rethinking. There is currently a lack of trust in key political institutions. Consider the latest findings of the Eurobarometer, an annual survey undertaken by the European Union (EU), which takes in the 27 countries of the EU. Taking those who trust from those who do not trust national governments, across the EU the figure is −35 per cent for governments (a significant negative finding); concerning each member state's parliaments it is −31 per cent.

When we look at the findings of the World Value Survey Association (Table 1), the picture is equally bleak. Respondents were asked how they rated democracy against their satisfaction with the way democracy is practiced in their respective countries. As Table 1 illustrates, their responses prove that across the world there is a gap between the perceived relative importance of democracy and the satisfaction with the performance of that democracy. The fact that some of the greatest dissatisfaction was expressed in North America and Western Europe reflects, one assumes, both the higher levels of expectation surrounding, and the importance placed on, democracy in those countries, but, equally, the sense that it is not fully delivering what it promises.

Table 1: Evidence of democratic deficit: Rating of importance of democracy against satisfaction with performance (out of 10)

Scandinavia	Net −1.53
Asia-Pacific	Net −1.55
South America	Net −1.78
Africa	Net −1.91
North America	Net −2.20
Western Europe	Net −2.25
Middle East	Net −2.96
Central and Eastern Europe	Net −2.96

Source: Pippa Norris and World Values Survey, 2005–2007; the democratic deficit is arrived at by calculating by the mean difference between the importance placed in the 'value of democracy' versus the assessment of how democratically the country was actually being governed at present. All of these regional clusters are negative indicating a deficit of actual performance.

Without discounting the variation in these figures, they suggest a general trend towards an established disengagement with politics. But really, it could be argued that this is nothing new — it's been a core feature of the way in which people have been thinking about democracy for three or four decades now. It is thus not a product of an immediate set of factors, rather, this mentality is ingrained in the way people think about democracy, and in many ways I think it reflects a wider feature of democracy: that democracy, as a collective form of decision-making, inevitably disappoints. This is because of the nature of the democratic promise, which gives citizens the right to engage on issues, but not the right to decide them.

The nature of the political process, which advantages compromise over truth, probably also explains this high level of civic cynicism. It can be argued that politics and politicians' behaviour contribute to the belief that democracy is somehow flawed.

In addition, there are three other factors that help explain the trend. One is the role of the media, particularly the way in which it frames politics and political choice, often in a simplistical and negative manner. Another is the breaking down of the control and influence that political parties have had over partisanship and the way in which people think about issues. Although this factor is perhaps less developed in Australia than in other liberal democracies, it is a feature of the Australian system. This also reflects the imbalance between performance delivery and expectations, in that citizens expect more from government itself, even though its diversity of interests and engagements stretch its capacity to deliver. An example can be seen in the efforts of UK Prime Minister David Cameron to appeal to citizens through his so-called 'happiness agenda.' The idea that happiness should be a metric against which governments measure their performance is stretching towards insanity.

While the idea of measuring a country's wealth other than through simple measures of gross domestic product is an important one, the presentation of the 'happiness agenda' is spectacularly silly. I am not sure, either, that governments are necessarily equipped to lead the discussion on this issue, because of the risk that, just because a government is talking about something, it is assumed they are taking responsibility for it.

There's no such thing as an 'average citizen'

Having established the idea that we are in a debate, and that it is a difficult debate because of the contemporary atmosphere of anti-politics, I will now explore my third theme: that there is no such thing as an average citizen. To frame this I ask a simple question of the reader: is apathy a choice? Obviously, in some senses it is, in that any rational person would be apathetic about some of the issues they are confronting — people clearly care about some issues more than others, and governments identify literally thousands of issues as open for discussion and debate. This variation in level of interest is known in the political science faternity as the 'intensity preference'.

Consequently, it should not be surprising to us that people do not express an interest in every issue that government identifies for discussion and debate. And yet, if apathy was simply a choice, then surely across the spectrum of society we wouldn't find evidence that there were some people participating to a much lesser degree than other people in the political process, because such engagement would be distributed according to intensities of preference. On other issues, conversely, those who previously had not engaged would be found to engage, even though there would be no systematic pattern to non-engagement.

Confused? I would not have made the ridiculous statement above unless I had some evidence that told me it was completely wrong and that inequalities in participation are significant. Therefore, apathy is as much constructed as it is a choice.

Below is some data which illustrates the scale of political disengagement that British people have in their heads. It is one of the rare surveys that asks people not only what they had done, but what they might do, using a whole range of political acts there as a measurement of this correlation between deed and desire. What is particularly interesting is that when it comes to the more substantial acts like attending a political meeting, taking part in a demonstration or forming a group of like-minded people, the gap between what people have actually done and what they might think about doing is substantial. What that tells us is that there is a potential for engagement and for participation which is not yet being delivered on.

Table 2: What British citizens do and what they might do

	Response rate	
Activity	**% Had done**	**% Would do**
Donated money	61.6	74.6
Voted in a local government election	51.7	71.5
Signed a petition	41.0	75.1
Boycotted certain products	30.5	57.4
Raised funds for an organisation	28.6	53.5
Bought for ethical reasons	26.9	47.4
Contacted a public official	25.1	58.8
Worn a campaign badge	21.1	17.7
Contacted a solicitor	19.1	58.4
Contacted a politician	13.3	53.0
Contacted an organisation	11.4	49.6
Contacted the media	8.6	41.9
Attended a political meeting	5.1	25.0
Taken part in a demonstration	4.4	32.0
Formed a group of like-minded people	4.4	22.0
Taken part in a strike	2.2	21.9
Participated in an illegal protest	1.4	11.5

Source: Citizen Audit of Great Britain 2000–2001.

Table 3: Income and participation — European evidence

Activity	Household's total net income, all sources									
	1st decile	2nd decile	3rd decile	4th decile	5th decile	6th decile	7th decile	8th decile	9th decile	10th decile
Contacted politician or official	10.8	11.8	12.7	12.3	14.8	15.1	16.5	18.8	20.1	23.9
Worked in political party	2.2	2.7	3.0	2.9	3.4	3.4	3.8	4.7	5.4	5.4
Worked in another political agency	9.1	11.8	11.7	14.4	16.0	16.9	21.6	22.0	22.2	25.2
Worn or displayed political badge	6.0	5.8	6.5	7.3	8.4	9.1	11.8	12.2	13.5	13.1
Signed petition, last 12 months	18.5	19.0	20.7	23.0	26.6	26.8	30.0	33.2	34.8	38.1
Taken part in lawful public demonstration	4.3	4.9	5.9	6.4	7.5	7.6	6.9	8.6	8.2	7.9
Boycotted certain products	14.2	14.1	14.1	15.2	19.8	23.0	24.3	27.0	26.7	32.5
Member of political party	3.2	4.1	3.2	4.4	4.7	4.4	4.8	4.7	5.9	5.6

Source: European Social Survey, 2006–08.

The evidence on inequality comes from the European Social Survey and draws upon 24 countries, running their income levels against various forms of political activity. It is not necessary to study the data in detail to see evidence of the trend: lower income levels equate with lower levels of participation, whereas higher income levels lead to higher levels of participation. It's a strong pattern, and there's no doubt that it's an important one too.

Table 4 offers another approach to this subject, using UK data for the Hansard Society. Grades A and B denote the professional and managerial classes, grades D and E the working classes. Obviously differences exist between these groups across a whole series of measures. These differences are in many ways more pronounced than those between men and women or between majority and minority communities. There are significant differences regarding the level of activism; for example, if you're an A or B kind of person, you're five times more likely to be counted as a political activist, compared to a D or E person.

Table 4: Social factors and participation, United Kingdom

Political factor % of	Social grade AB	Social grade DE	Men	Women	White	BME (black and minority ethnic)
Interest	77	36	63	53	60	41
Knowledge	73	29	63	43	54	39
Activist	25	5	12	15	14	5
Voting	72	43	57	59	60	44
Efficacy	31	30	31	29	29	38

Source: Developed from data in the Hansard Society Audit of Political Engagement, 2011. Ipsos MORI.

There are also some other interesting distinctions. Take the finding that men have 63 per cent knowledge of politics, compared to women at 43 per cent of knowledge. As the more detailed work went on to prove, however, this was simply because men were more boastful about the knowledge that they had (again, not a major insight).

Some new insights into citizen engagement with the political process

Some fascinating work about how different personality types might be inclined to engage with politics in different ways has also been conducted. There is also interesting work being done on the role of emotion, particularly anger, in driving people's participation in and engagement with the political process. Again, this is a significant issue if you try and frame participation as some kind of managerial solution, especially if it turns out that people have to get angry before they engage. And, finally, we also know that friendship networks and networks of people who are acquainted with politics play a significant role in driving political engagement and encouraging people who may otherwise be apathetic about politics to show interest in a particular political issue.

Another issue that deserves further research is what exactly are the problems citizens' have with politics and the representative process. Current attempts to determine this involve focus groups exploring what people find problematic or alienating about politics and why they find engagement with it difficult.

While the above research will help in our understanding of public participation in the political process, the standard starting point remains recognition that socioeconomic variables influence inequalities of political engagement.

Systems need to cope with diversity; some research has been conducted on how to engage with hard-to-reach groups and how to ensure that they are involved in the political process. More generally, when considering systems of engagement, those that are direct, straightforward and simple tend to display less bias. In other words, the differential between somebody being asked to vote, as opposed to somebody who spends a huge amount of time on deliberating about it, is one where voting would tend to show less inequality and less difference. As we already know, different forms of non-partisan engagement are attractive to people who won't engage in mainstream politics. Thus, creating different opportunities for people to engage seems to be the most obvious way to address issues of inequality.

An audit tool to enable public authorities to consider methods and levels of participation among stakeholders has been developed by myself, in collaboration with Lawrence Pratchett and Vivien Lowndes. A framework, which was produced to support this tool and influenced by the CLEAR framework (see Table 5), is being used extensively in Europe and some parts of Australia.

Table 5: CLEAR — an audit framework

Factor	Audit check	Policy response
Can do	The resources that people have as well as confidence to use them	Capacity building aimed at individuals or communities
Like to	A sense of involvement with the public entity that is the focus of engagement	Sense of community, civic engagement, social capital and citizenship
Enabled to	The civic infrastructure of organisations that organise participation.	To support the civic infrastructure: a set of viable civic institutions.
Asked to	Mobilising people into participation by asking for their input can make a big difference	Public participation schemes that are diverse and reflexive
Responded to	Participate if they are listened to and able to see a response	A public policy system that can show a capacity to respond

Source: V. Lowndes, L. Pratchett and G. Stoker 'Diagnosing and Remedying the Failings of Official Participation Schemes: The CLEAR framework', *Social Policy & Society*, v. 5:2, pp. 1–11, 2006.

The CLEAR features are likely to be familiar to the reader: the 'Can do' feature relates strongly to the socioeconomic features; 'like to' signifies that people have to feel they're part of a community that is entitled to be asked; 'enable to' and 'ask to' reflect the sense in which people are mobilised and the way that they are approached; and, finally and crucially, if we are going to make participation work, people have to be responded to (the 'r' in CLEAR). This system is useful for testing who is engaged, who isn't engaged and what the factors are that drive disengagement or engagement in certain stakeholders or communities.

Along with other colleagues, I also have a new piece of work that frames interventions under the broad headings 'nudge' and 'think'. The 'nudge' component reflects how individuals can be approached, framing information in social cues, so as to help them do things for themselves in society. 'Think', on the other hand, captures another tradition of approaching citizens through more deliberative and collective forms of engagement. We think that a combination of 'nudge' and 'think' could make a real difference, in terms of encouraging engagement.

Obviously, the idea of 'nudge' and 'think' were created to facilitate another naff title; the book *Nudge, Nudge, Think, Think* was published by Bloomsbury in September 2011 and authored by myself, Peter John, Sarah Cotterill, Alice Moseley, Liz Richardson, Graham Smith and Corinne Wales.

In this book we tested the 'nudge' and 'think' interventions using randomised controlled trials. The 'nudge' approach is based on insights from behavioural science, particularly from behavioural psychology, about how it is that people approach decision-making in an irrational (or not fully rational) manner, but they are informed by cognitive and social cues in order to enable them to make decisions.

The approach then assumes that people are relatively smart decision-makers; that they can shift their behavior according to the way in which information and social messages are conveyed to them. For example, if you give them rapid feedback, or give them social information about what others are doing, or you encourage them to make a pledge, you can change their behaviour. A series of interventions tested this philosophy and it was evident that nudges work; so there is definitely something in 'nudge' and definitely something in the insights that come from behavioural science in terms of approaching people differently and giving consideration to their processes of decision-making. This leads to better outcomes. There are normative challenges involved in 'nudge' because this intervention involves an element of trickery in that the individual is being persuaded to do something without being fully informed of the context in which they do it. Even so, I think that the evidence suggests it can be decisive in changing peoples' minds.

Most of our nudges worked in a modest, rather than transformative, way. For example, during our research we created nudges that encouraged people to recycle more; as a consequence, recycling rates increased by five to seven per cent. We also designed a nudge that encourage people to volunteer more. We did this by persuading a particular local authority, when faced with a phone complaint, to reply (after addressing the complaint) in the manner of 'You sound like a person that knows quite a bit about your community. Would you like to volunteer to help out within your community?' Though the local authorities took some persuasion to do that (because they thought people would slam down the phone in response), eight out of 10 complainers said yes, they would like to volunteer. Indeed, a problem arose from having such a positive response because the local authority didn't have enough things for people to volunteer to do.

We have nudged people into signing up to organ donation lists and into voting, and our research indicates that there is a whole series of different ways in which you can persuade people to take a more significant civic responsibility, even if the shift is modest rather than transformative. In this sense we are looking at modest shifts; say from 20 per cent doing something to 70 per cent doing it.

Much of our evidence suggests that both nudge and think tend to work best when driven locally, rather than from a top-down perspective. The reason why nudge works more effectively on a local level is that it can only succeed if you trust the source of the nudge. And as research shows, people are more likely to trust institutions close to their community, so it makes sense they are more likely to be nudged on a local level.

The issue of whether people participate and engage at a local rather than a national level is more complicated. A narrow focus on neighbourhoods and communities misunderstands the way that citizens currently define locality. If you think about the lives most citizens lead, the notion of locality is now much more diverse and expansive than it was 20 or 30 years ago. Consider factors like the journey to work, shopping and leisure opportunities — the facilities to which individuals have access. Though they are 'local' in the contemporary context, they are potentially spread over a much wider area than they used to be. And, of course, there is the Internet, which creates communities of interest as opposed to communities of place.

We must, therefore, recognise the need to penetrate these felt communities while being careful not to assume they are always based on a street, or a neighbourhood, or a residence. In other words, we need to take locality seriously, but not narrowly define it around a small residential community.

There is an online resource devoted to this subject, currently under construction. Graham Smith is involved with people from a range of universities in making a website called Participedia Net — a kind of Wikipedia for those interested in participation. It will be invaluable for gathering people's knowledge and information and participation initiatives. It will also allow people to contribute their own findings on the topic and host relevant discussions.

This leads to my final point about new forms of engagement: there seems to be no answer without the Internet, which has the capacity for rapid mobilisation and influence. It is clearly part of the way in which citizens are doing things and its attraction is that it lowers barriers to engagement.

I do, however, have some cautionary remarks to make about the Internet. It can be divisive and there are issues preventing its effective use as a deliberative forum. For example, one of our experiments involved an online component, for which we received substantial participation. Over 6000 people engaged in an online discussion about how to deal with anti-social behavior and 25 per cent of the participants made a significant contribution to the discussion and debate. While there was notable participation, it was evident that people entered discussions and debates in which they agreed with content posted by others; individuals sought to reinforce their opinions by accessing sympathetic online content.

Concluding thoughts

I have two concluding thoughts. The first is that in the area of citizen engagement, it is important to recognise that systems have been dominated by professionals and experts and this creates the problem of unaccountable bureaucrats. You could then say, 'well, let citizens decide,' but that potentially leads to the tyranny of the majority. Or, you could say, 'we should have specialised lobby groups and producers deciding', but that leads to the problem of self-interested particularism. Equally, the dominance of elected politicians deciding creates the problem of a construction of politics within the machine, an institutional setting that, in some sense, divorces politicians from the rest of society.

Constructing an effective and successful democracy is challenging and difficult, but it is essential to give real democracy a chance. If we take the recent example of phone-hacking undertaken by staff of Rupert Murdoch's daily UK paper *News of the World*, what he did was confuse populism with democracy; he forgot that democracy involves informed engagement and participation where you take the views of others seriously. If you believe any of Murdoch's output in the United Kingdom was committed to that, then you saw it in a different way to me.

The Murdoch scandal illustrates how difficult it is to hold powerful people to account — a crucial, underpinning feature of a democracy. To achieve such accountability in a complex constitutional settlement it is necessary to have independence in the judiciary and public servants, who implement decisions and provide expertise to politicians.

But in terms of the balancing role of citizen engagement, it is fundamental that we go much further than the current system does for one main reason: to combat the threat of fascism. Over the past 20 years Europe has seen a marked rise in right wing populist politics, a trend premised on the commonly held opinion that democracy is failing because it is not delivering any real sense of control over people's lives, and because it is allowing rich and powerful people to get away with whatever they choose, simply because they have cosy relationships with elected politicians.

The Murdoch episode brought those issues to the fore and reasserted the necessity of taking democracy seriously in order to ensure that it does not become too populist. It would be naive to imagine that people will engage all the time, however, it is important to take seriously the notion that democracy should deliver for the average citizen — the feeling that democracy works for them, rather than for other people.

We need a democracy that requires those that are powerful to take responsibility, as well as putting responsibility onto those who are less powerful. We also need a democracy that builds cohesion as well as reconciling division. The challenges, then, are significant, but they can be met if we — as public servants but also as citizens — try and encourage a much wider and much more genuine democracy. The solution is to take democracy seriously, rather than put up with the thin and rather pathetic form of democracy that has dominated in the majority of the world's liberal democracies.

References

Norris, Pippa, 2011. *Democratic Deficits: Critical citizens revisited*, Cambridge University Press, New York.

3. Beyond New Public Management: Will governments let citizens and communities determine policy choices and service mixes?

Don Kettl

On a previous trip to Australia, some 15 years ago, I had a conversation with academics and practitioners about the idea of putting citizens at the centre of policy-making processes. This topic frames my contribution to this volume of essays. Are governments really ready to let go of their hold on the policymaking process? The simple answer is 'no'. The bigger problem is whether citizens are ready to step up — and the answer to that question is 'maybe'.

There is a transformation currently underway which will bring citizens into the decision-making process and adjust to the realities of governance in the 21st century. The success of this transformation, however, requires us to address two important issues.

The first is whether we are essentially at the end of a phase of citizen engagement in government, and whether new ideas are surfacing. The second is how this issue is playing out in nations around the world.

We have spent two generations betting on expanding the role of citizens in government. One of the enormous breakthroughs and contributions to the philosophy of new public management (NPM) was the idea that government is too disconnected from citizens and not responsive enough to their needs. By finding a way to make government more efficient and more responsive, the movement suggested, we could forge a fundamental change in the way in which government operates. We have now spent a significant amount of time attempting to advance this movement. This has been accelerated by the 24-hour news cycle, which has made it impossible for anybody to go anywhere without being connected constantly to what is happening elsewhere.

Compared with the 1980s, when NPM was first being adopted, the connection between citizens and government is now easier to follow. When I visited Australia recently I was able to follow on television not only the Australian perspective on US financial problems, but also the live debates occurring halfway around the world in Washington DC. And when I return to the United States, I can similarly watch political events occurring in Australia and New Zealand.

There are three vignettes that help make this point. Consider Michelle Bachmann, who was for a time a leading candidate for the Republican nomination in the 2012 US presidential election. She is a leader of the Tea Party movement and has said that it is time 'for tough love for the American government'. She emphasised 'I will not raise taxes, I will reduce spending and I will not vote to raise the debt ceiling'. The Tea Party movement has roots in the United States, going back to the 1770s when American revolutionaries dressed up as American Indians to invade British ships. By throwing tea into the harbour in Boston, they helped spark not just opposition to taxes but rebellion against British rule.

Unlike Australia and New Zealand, Americans decided 200 years ago to go to war to end the rule of the British crown. The constitutional system that was devised as a result made it hard for anyone to do anything quickly — and sometimes to do anything at all. Australians and New Zealanders have been more patient and have maintained more confidence in government.

The Tea Party movement has tapped into a reservoir of concern in the United States about the essence of government. In the United States, there are powerful arguments that we have too much government; that it is time to downsize and shrink government. Government considers citizen engagement to be a key step towards this end, but other measures are necessary. In the United States and around the world, we are nearing a major tipping point. A recent article in the *Economist* opined that 'Australians must now decide what sort of country they want their children to live in' ('Australia's Promise: The next golden state', 26 May 2011). The debate is not only about the size of government, but what it is that government ought to be. In a recent question time in the New Zealand parliament, a parliamentarian referred to the forum as increasingly ineffectual and cynical: 'I worry that it [question time] is turning into a contest to see who can make the most noise. Question time is not about that'. The United States does not have question time — a blessing, considering that existing US policy debates are similarly tense and cynical.

Against this bleak backdrop, the connection between citizens and government is important. Citizen engagement is now, however, about much more than co-production. It has evolved far beyond the aim of improving efficiency. Increasingly, the focus is on the identity and values of governments: who we are, what we want to be, and how we are going to achieve our objectives. This is just as fundamental as it was at the beginning of the NPM movement.

Over the last decades, there have been improvements in the efficiency of government around the world because of the reforms introduced by NPM. But, despite these efforts, there has been a decline in support for public institutions. And, in the aftermath of recent economic collapse, tight fiscal constraints will remain for some time. The idea of going back to normal, as many people hoped in late 2008, seems to be a pipedream. In the United States there is a phrase about the 'new normal', with fiscal constraints now the inescapable imperative of our age. That, in turn, is driving the sense of what it is we want government to do.

Democrats are now talking about cuts, and they are battling Republicans to see who can downsize government the most. We are talking about a radical reshaping of what it is the government does in a way that also simultaneously holds out demands for better performance. People might not like or trust government much, but every problem that emerges quickly becomes a public problem.

Recently I participated in a panel discussion about the 2010 BP oil spill in the Gulf of Mexico. This was an unusual public problem in that the oil rig was owned by BP, a private company, and it blew up beyond American waters. Despite this being a failure of a private company in international waters, the public immediately looked to the government to step in and solve the problem. We might hear from citizens that they want less government and fewer taxes, but, when a problem arises, we expect instant response from government.

Consider the levels of trust in government in the United States (or lack thereof). The technical explanation is not a happy story. In 1960, trust in government was relatively high. It fell during the Vietnam War and hit a low point in 1980. During the presidency of Ronald Reagan, trust began to grow but it collapsed again in the 1990s. In the aftermath of the terrorist attacks on the United States in 2001, and the continuing policy gridlock that prevails in Washington, public trust and confidence in government has declined again. Polling suggests that people really do not much like or trust President Barak Obama, but they dislike and trust the Republicans even more.

Other nations speak of hung parliaments; in the United States, there are a lot of people who would like to hang the parliament. At this point, there is a sense that nobody is in charge. The system of government requires everybody to work together, but nobody wants to work on anything. I do not believe that this is because our representatives are nasty people; rather, they are good people whose wide range of views militates against them achieving compromise in an increasingly constrained political system. The tense and cynical atmosphere in Washington is, therefore, less about particular policy debates and more a crisis about what government is and what citizens' relationship to that government will be. Distrust in government is not just an American problem, but it is certainly higher in that country than in most Western democracies.

So, during the NPM era, fundamental issues have been confronted, but continue to require resolution. A series of management reforms have been implemented in an effort to try to sort these issues out. Public sectors have been transformed according to a theory that the things government should do can be assigned to agencies to produce those results. We put leaders in charge and held them accountable for their outputs and ultimately for the outcomes. We have been spending roughly the last 20 years trying to put boundaries around problems and trying to make those boundaries work more effectively. Now we struggle to connect those boxes more with citizens.

In the Westminster approach to these government reforms, there has been a focus on making departmental managers more accountable. At the same time, however, there has been an increasing realisation that agencies need to work with each other across agency boundaries. Consequently, we now grapple with a puzzle of how to prevent the boundaries around the agencies from frustrating the ability of managers to manage effectively and prevent them complicating the problem of coordinating action. That puzzle has begun to collide with the logic of the reforms that have been underway for the last 15 or 20 years.

Then there is the American approach, which is based on letting the managers manage; liberating managers to be able to do what it is that they intuitively know should be done. This philosophy has collided with incredible political pressures (where politicians seek to meddle) and in turn has created strong incentives for managers simply to keep their heads down to avoid having them shot off in the tough political battle.

In short, we have reached an end of reform, in two respects. First, we have reached the end of the logical progression of what we have been working on for the last 15 or 20 years in the public sector. We have done moderately well, but we have now reached the point where the reforms that we launched have gone as far as they can. Second, we are now struggling to redefine the purpose of our reform endeavours. What is government's role in reform in the 21st century and how are we going to make that work?

This is a very tough set of questions that goes far beyond the framework that has driven reforms for the last 15 years.

We have produced some dramatic gains, but we have also placed more boundaries between agencies along the way. Can you think of any problem that matters that any one organisation can control? I have not found anyone who can come up with even one example. And if that is the case, we will increasingly depend on the ability of agencies to connect with each other. That flies in the face of the reforms that have compartmentalised problems and required agencies to respond to them within their boundaries.

A related approach depends on information. I was recently at a meeting in Washington with a senior bureaucrat in the Obama administration, who admitted that the administration was collecting and distributing vast amounts of information — but he wasn't sure that anybody read or used the information they produced. In the information age, we know that information matters. But we do not know how to produce information that matters or with which citizens can effectively engage.

In addition is the importance of our notion of the 'big idea'. When I visited Australia in 1995, I was not only struck that there was a driving idea called the 'NPM', but also that there was a literature on it, intellectual excitement about it, and a sense that something really big was afoot. Look around now and ask yourself: what is the current 'big idea'? There is a consensus, I think, that NPM has done a lot of very important work but that it has run its course. People are looking for the next big idea, but there is currently no idea that will galvanise action as the NPM did when it was launched in New Zealand in the late 1980s.

Another problem is that the public has higher expectations for immediate results, but it is also less prepared to make the sacrifices needed to achieve them. Within government there is a sense that governments are too wasteful, and need to be downsized, but there is also greater resistance by civil servants to proposed cuts to their programs.

Citizens do not understand the necessities of reform, and politicians are too scared to tell citizens that their expectations are unreasonable. This is at the core of the question about what it is that people really expect from government. It is a major unresolved question in the United States and, I think, it is increasingly becoming so in many countries around the world. It is now accentuated by fiscal stress, which shows no signs of going away. We cannot rely on economic growth to solve this dilemma. And it is hard for the public to trust government to solve the problem because they do not tend to trust the government with big questions.

We are at a historically important moment in which we are facing some tough constraints, without a big idea to drive us, but with the inescapable necessity to solve our problems. I believe in improving customer satisfaction, in trying to create better one-stop shops, in integrating government services, and in making government more transparent. Those things are important, but we are at the point where we are making only marginal improvements that will not suffice to solve our problems and citizens' demands.

Considering this bleak portrayal, it is hard to be optimistic about our governments' ability to reform to meet its citizens' immediate expectations and address critical long-term problems. Hence, it is worth asking whether we are satisfied with what we have now — and whether what we have is as good as it is going to get. What does it mean to engage citizens in government and can we give them what they want? Are they willing to pay for what they want? And if we are going to continue doing what we are doing, are we going to be able to do it any better than we are now?

One of the problems is that, in the United States and indeed globally, the current political atmosphere focuses on government mistakes; there are rarely compliments for good government performance. There is no kind of expectation that the public will reward high performance, because that is why citizens pay government. The result is that government becomes risk-averse; its policy outlook more short-term. Administrators replicate this cautious behaviour by performing business as usual.

That takes us to the final puzzle about how we can bring citizens in. Consider the example of governments since the middle ages operating programs to eliminate rat infestations. During the 1910s, Philadelphia had a special 'rat receiving station', with a rat patrol wagon that would cruise the city. A more modern version of this, the 'Rat Rub-out Program', was created by the mayor of Baltimore in the early years of the 21st century.

The program encouraged citizens to telephone a call centre to report any kind of problem, whether it be a hole in the road, sidewalk cracks — or rat infestations. When citizens called in with reports of rat infestations, the city captured the locations and mapped the areas with rat clusters. Figure 1 maps the calls received about rat problems: areas with a high concentration of rats are marked by green; these spots become darker and darker where there are more reports of bigger rats.

The next question was: if rats are a public health problem, and citizens expect government to get rid of them, how can governments achieve this? Create a department of rats? The notion of creating a new agency is, of course, absurd. The responsibility for rat infestations rests with various agencies — the Department of Health, sanitation and rubbish pick-up services, and housing agencies (because rats tend to live in abandoned buildings and, if you have too many abandoned houses, rubbish will accumulate). Delegating responsibility for exterminating rats, then, becomes a difficult task.

The solution lay in ensuring that all of the agencies with a share of the rat problem worked together. Of course, the standard approach to collaboration is this: the mayor orders everyone to collaborate; everyone says yes, then goes back to the office and nothing changes. But in Baltimore, the mayor took personal leadership, constantly monitoring the data and charts on rat infestations. It became difficult for managers to walk away from the problem because there were clear accountability measures.

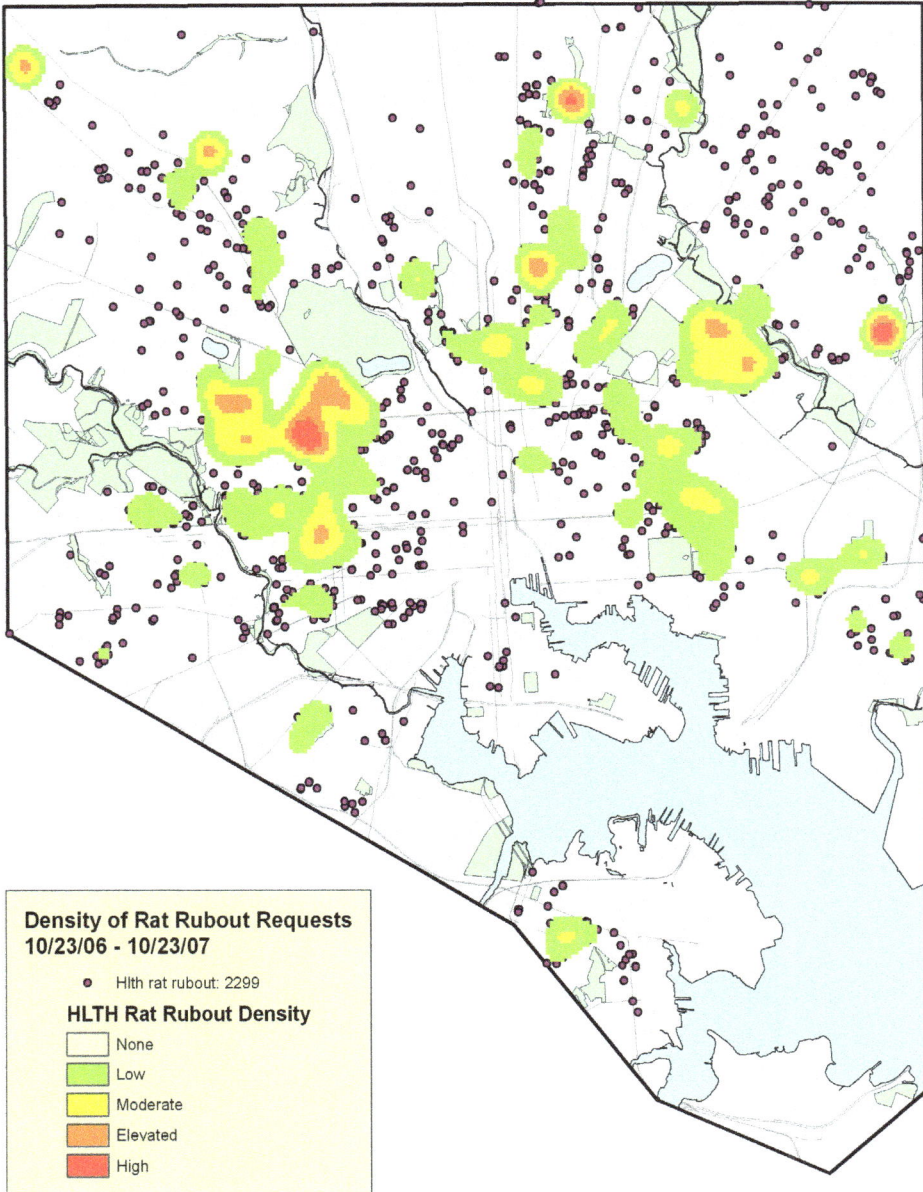

**Density of Rat Rubout Requests
10/23/06 - 10/23/07**

● Hlth rat rubout: 2299

HLTH Rat Rubout Density

	None
	Low
	Moderate
	Elevated
	High

Figure 1: Rat Rub-out

Source: www.baltimorecity.gov/news/citistat/reports.html

Another example of cross-agency program delivery occurred in the aftermath of the economic crisis, when the US federal government created an $US800 billion public stimulus program. The US administration's worry was that there would be manifold opportunities for fraud and waste, so it decided to track the money. But the administration went further: not only would *they* track the money, they made it possible for everyone else to do so by allowing anybody, anywhere, to follow what projects were going on in their street through an online mapping program. In fact, I can check on these data with my iPhone, through an app that the government designed. As a result, an $800 billion program can be tracked to each citizen's address.

When users examine the community programs through the online mapping system, they see that one is run by a job training agency, one by a housing agency or one by a community services agency. I showed one of these charts to a first-year college student. Within 30 seconds, she asked the most important question: I wonder if they talk to each other? Once you chart the location of such numerous projects, the question of coordination becomes inescapable, because you are not only talking about programs or agencies but about neighbourhoods. You are talking about how government interacts to affect people where they live. You have accountability that operates by place and not by agency or program. It becomes impossible to walk away from the question of whether there's another program two blocks away that is very similar, run by a different agency that requires coordination. If we are interested in place-based performance, coordination becomes inescapable.

The primary concern remains whether or not anybody cares about accessing this information. Either way, giving citizens access to real-time, place-based data — not data on what happened last year or the year before or five years ago — is an accountability measure that will improve our chances of successfully engaging citizens.

The second issue is a need to redefine outcome indicators. The elimination of rat infestations should not be seen as an outcome in itself; rather, the outcome depends on a range of related factors. For example, substandard housing and dilapidated conditions in inner cities are hotspots for rat populations, therefore rats cannot be eliminated without improving housing conditions and, indeed, the overall quality of the neighbourhood. Relentless follow-up by leaders will be crucial in reinforcing this approach.

The third issue is a need to redefine accountability. Instead of traditional compliance accountability we need a new approach that focuses on the quality of services for citizens. The issue then becomes not so much making an agency or program work better, but making the neighbourhood in which citizens live work better. Having accountability and management focused on place is a revolutionary concept. Readers who understand NPM know that this explodes many of the underlying arguments. Its goal is to change the conversation so that it can crack the dilemmas of accountability.

Leadership is a crucial part of this new paradigm, and some points on this subject must be made. Firstly, and paradoxically, in the increasing complexity of the state, the role of individual leaders becomes more important. As part of NPM we have spent time trying to formulate constructs that encourage leaders to lead, but not investing much in our understanding of the importance of the leader per se. And it turns out that, in so doing, we have reached the limits of this insular approach, because the new types of leaders needed are the ones that are accomplished in reaching out.

The United States learned this lesson from its experience during Hurricane Katrina. The response to the hurricane was chaotic and the initial phase failed largely because of efforts to manage the program within agency boundaries. Solutions began to be found when leaders arrived and started to understand what the problem was, not while they remained off-site, managing the federal agency in charge of emergency response. There were people who were stuck on rooftops and needed to be rescued, and an effective response required cross-agency collaboration and a lot of spontaneous thinking from leaders.

In many ways this is the crucial aspect of the engagement issue. Most American citizens don't know which agency will be in charge of a problem that affects them, they don't particularly care; they just want the government to respond and one of the government's problems is trying to figure out how to connect 'the problem' and 'the need for response' to the people who are going to be responsible for fixing it. The fixers, however, often lie in multiple agencies and so government's second layer problem is trying to figure out how to weave that together. Ultimately, even if citizens do not know and do not care about knowing which government agencies are responsible for addressing their problems, the government must continue with the major reforms addressed in this chapter, even in the current austere financial environment.

But there are a couple of final things to note. Service coordination may be one way of providing some reassurance to citizens that government is listening and connecting, and there are some things that are high priority and high visibility. In America, when regions are affected by snow storms, big potholes in the middle of the road or other things that annoy people, it is reassuring to know that the officials responsible for fixing these problems are taking their roles seriously and providing guarantees to fix the problems. The kind of service coordination that is required is instructive. It potentially provides a way for public officials to talk more honestly with the citizens about what it is that has to happen.

The ongoing and proposed reforms described in this chapter are by no means certain to be the 'next big things'. But two things seem clear. First, doing more of the same is going to produce more of the same results. The declining trust in government and rising fiscal constraints would guarantee that. Second, framing today's challenges as a problem of performance and accountability, with information as the driver changing incentives, is an interesting approach that offers some hope.

The first part of this chapter might have been depressing — we do face significant challenges in government. But the second half offers significant hope. We are in the middle of a radical and exciting transformation that gives us the chance to rethink what government is, how it works and, most importantly, how it connects with citizens. Increasingly it appears that government is less in the business of delivering services per se and more in the business of weaving together integrative responses to public problems, where some of the solutions are governmental, some lie in the private sector and others in the non-governmental sector. This is an opportunity to increase government productivity which may not be possible to achieve in any other way.

4. Citizens and Governments: Getting closer or further apart?

Rolf Alter

Whether governments connect with their citizens and how they do so is, as it has been in the past, a prominent subject in the public governance debate across the group of Organisation for Economic Co-operation and Development (OECD) nations. The 2011 Australia and New Zealand School of Government (ANZSOG) national conference on 'Putting Citizens First: Engagement in Policy and Service Delivery for the 21st Century' is a prominent example of taking a fresh look at a known subject. Answering the question of why there is such renewed interest requires consideration of several issues.

Unfinished business of managing engagement

Previous arguments and discussions around 'citizens first', 'focus on citizens' or 'citizen-centered government' have remained inconclusive to a large extent. In a recent comprehensive assessment by the OECD, *Focus on Citizens: Public engagement for better policy and services*,[1] participating countries reported mixed progress in applying the 'guiding principles' for information, consultation and active participation in policy-making which had been developed by the OECD in 2001. Overall, governments appear to have concluded that they had established rights, had active citizens and had a commitment to engage them in policy-making, but faced challenges of resources, time and lack of evaluation (Figure 1).

The report identified a number of remaining challenges for governments that do not seem to have lost any relevance in ensuing years since the publication's release. These include:

- How to design cost effective and useful public consultation and engagement initiatives.
- How to make public policy more interesting and relevant to more people.
- How to earn and keep people's trust that government will actually use their input.

---

1   OECD. 2009. *Focus on Citizens: Public engagement for better policy and services*. Paris.

- How to address the time constraints that characterise modern urban societies in OECD countries.
- How to raise the impact of evaluation on ongoing learning and continuous quality improvement of participation processes.

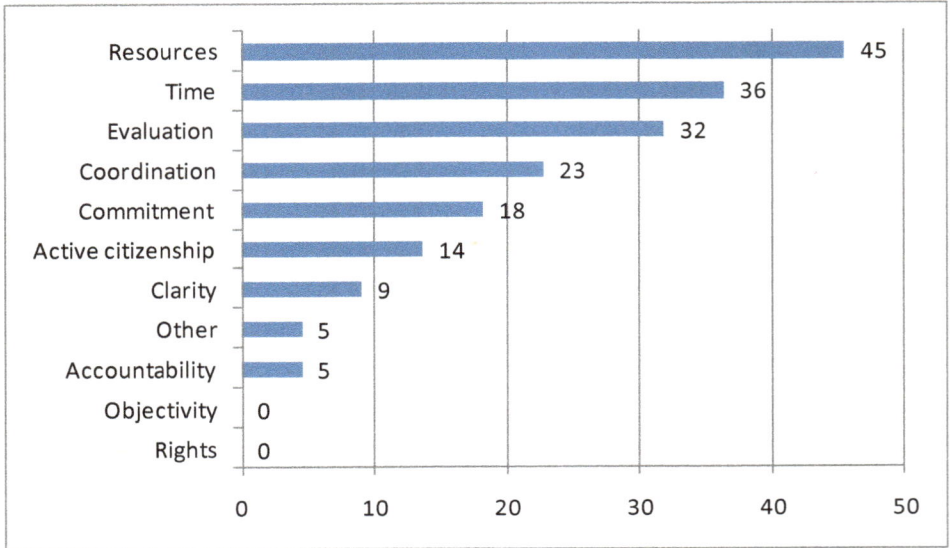

Figure 1: Principles which are the most difficult to meet (% respondents, n=25 countries)

% respondents ranking the option as 'important' or 'very important'.

Source: OECD. 2009. *Focus on Citizens: Public engagement for better Policy and services*. Paris.

New opportunities through information technology

The answers to some of these questions may be found in recent information technology (IT) developments. The rapidly accelerating promise of IT to provide an unlimited potential of dialogue and interaction with citizens is making electronic-based initiatives a standard feature of most— if not all — public sector reform programs. An overview of country initiatives published by the OECD,[2] pointed to growing expectations for technology and social media to be a critical channel for governments to inform their citizens, as well as facilitating citizens' access to government.

---

2 OECD. 2011. *The Call for Innovative and Open Government: An overview of country initiatives*. Paris.

Despite some progress, however, challenges remain. Effectively mobilising citizens around policy design and service delivery requires: solutions for the associated implications for the back office, the effective monitoring of citizen mobilisation, and the demonstration to citizens of a return by government to a focus on the quality of policy performance. The search for and exchange of positive experiences in responding to these challenges are important tasks that are still to be addressed.

Changes in the economic and social environment

Revisiting the government–citizen relationship would be incomplete without taking into account other important associated developments, some of them relatively recent. Such examples include:

- The 'Arab Spring' of 2011, in which citizen awakening in Tunisia and Egypt subsequently spread throughout North Africa, the Middle East, and eventually to Europe and the United States. Such 'global indignation'[3] is adding a new quality and quantity to the involvement of citizens with government.
- The call for a new balance between governments and markets which emerged in the wake of the economic crisis of 2008–2009, but seems to have fallen victim of powerful interests.
- The impact of fiscal consolidation on public policies to deliver growth and public services.

I would like to focus my comments on these three factors, as I believe they are particularly relevant in addressing the question of governments and citizens being driven apart or drawing closer together.

In these three case studies, one can easily identify arguments and observations that would support the hypothesis of a widening gulf between citizens and governments, as much as there are those that provide evidence of a closer relationship. Exploring these countervailing tendencies should help establish realistic expectations of governments, and encourage discussion of instruments and policies for greater dialogue, effective participatory policy design and more space for citizen involvement in service delivery. There may also be a need to assess some more fundamental implications for the future role of government and governance arrangements. Consider now the three case studies.

---

3   Gideon Rachman. 2011. *Financial Times*, 30 August, p. 7.

1. Citizen engagement: Now on their terms?

If there were any doubts about the potential, scope, willingness and ability of citizens to engage with governments, the awakening of Arab societies across the Middle East and North Africa in 2011 provides some forceful arguments against them. All the more so, as this so-called 'Arab Spring' (which lasted into summer, autumn and winter) is inspiring a growing number of citizen movements in other countries with diverse economic, social or political systems. In exploiting the potential of IT — including access to social media — citizens are organising themselves to reshape political debate, press for political decisions and even effectuate regime change. The participants in this 'global indignation' determine the terms of interaction with governments, connect in ways and by means of their choice and are proactive rather than reactive to invitations by governments for dialogue.

That isn't to say IT solutions are critical to the success or even presence of such movements. Powerful examples of effective citizen engagement arose long before the arrival of the information society as we experience it today, such as the many uprisings against Communist regimes in Eastern Europe. Moreover, not all today's movements are necessarily constructive in terms of policy design or better policies.

They all, however, are characterised by the fact that governments are no longer necessarily in the driver's seat of citizen engagement — nor do they have to be. This is not to belittle their serious and creative efforts to mobilise citizens through sophisticated consultation processes, open-government policies or co-operative ways of public service delivery. Data on outsourcing and co-production show that governments have in fact moved significant resources to buy or pay for non-government entities to provide 'public services' (Figure 2).

While governments are aware of citizens becoming increasingly sophisticated 'clients' of theirs, replicating their experience as consumers, the qualitative change to 'emancipated' citizens is probably a new phenomenon for most governments. Citizens not only set their own agenda, and demand policy action, they also suggest solutions and call for results from governments. More often than not, these are in time spans that are unfamiliar for almost all governments and public administrations.

Keeping up with the emancipated citizen is not only a challenge for the executive branch of governments. The traditional forms of democratic participation — be they through political parties, and the representation of citizens in parliaments — are facing similar challenges, including being bypassed, or having their monopoly as the voice of the people undermined.

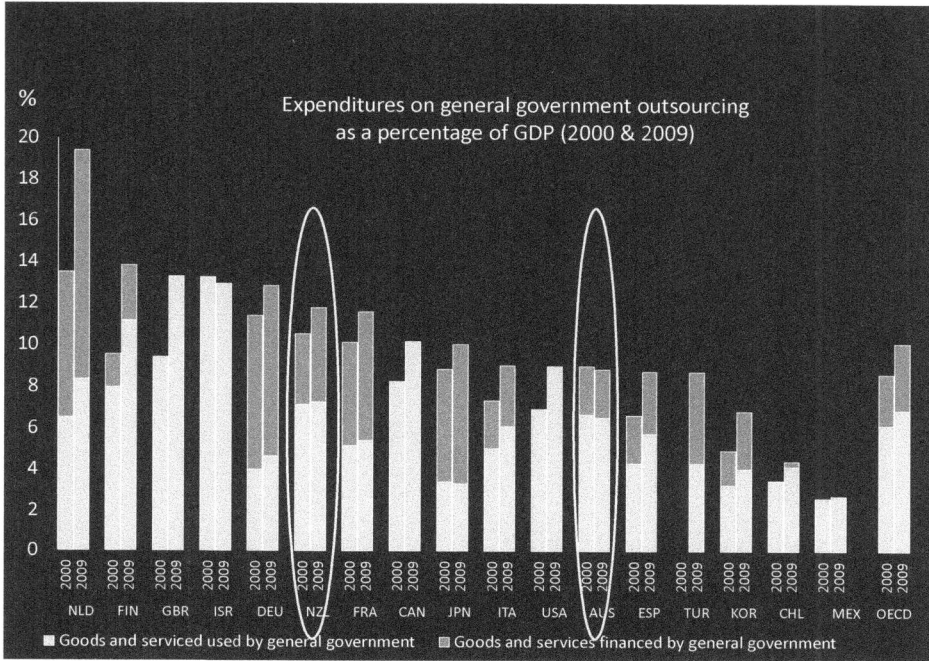

Figure 2: Expenditures on general government outsourcing as a percentage of GDP (2000 & 2009)

Source: Government at a Glance, OECD, 2011.

But is it only the emancipated citizen that challenges governments and parliaments? Vested interests and entrenched rent-seekers (i.e., actors who manipulate the political environment to extract 'economic rent' for themselves) have been joined by a range of other pressure groups, often so-called 'one-issue' movements. Lobby groups, or the media, are seen to exert a disproportionate influence over events.

In light of events that occurred across the Arab world in 2011, governments everywhere must ask themselves some important questions: How did we get to this awakening — beyond the facilitating factor of technology? How do we respond to legitimate and illegitimate pressures from vested interests? What are the implications for public policy design and public service delivery? How does it impact on the functioning of protective and/or developmental democracy which can be found in OECD countries, and how do we remedy any negative repercussions?

2. From modifying the 'social contract' to a new balance between markets and governments?

In the post-1945 world, across the OECD, the notion of the welfare state emerged with a priority to guarantee a minimum standard of living to all citizens through the provision of public services to all sectors of society. The social contract included the state's responsibility for preserving citizens' rights, guaranteeing social protection and ensuring civic liberties. While the exact terms of the social contract differed among countries, they all presented some mix of protective and developmental democracy.

The radical, very visible change in policies in the United Kingdom towards 'deregulation' of the economy in the 1970s could be interpreted as the starting point of a long term, gradual reduction of the role of the state in managing the economy and society. The neo-liberal school advocated and helped make reality a situation in which previously public goods became private ones, be it in the areas of public infrastructure of roads, railways, ports or airports, or in utilities, including telecommunications, water and power. At a later stage of this transition process, citizens were given the 'right to choose', or were entrusted with the responsibility to take care of their old age pensions, their health coverage or the education of their children.

While this growing privatisation of public services was driven by the promise of greater efficiency through private sector involvement, one may question whether it also contributed to a 'loser' relationship between citizens and government. With a multiplicity of service providers, the challenge of maintaining common standards in servicing citizens in health, education, security and safety emerged. Could citizens perceive government as abdicating its responsibilities, with important consequences in terms of their overall accountability?

If governments were no longer — or not to the same extent — guaranteeing access to public services, why should citizens' behaviour not change as well? If citizens were to interpret the gradual withdrawal of the state as an attempt to modify the social contract, governments would become just one of the players in the networks of individual citizens. Why then engage with the government more than with others? In fact, one could formulate the hypothesis that governments invented their commitment to 'focus on citizens' in response to the disenfranchisement of citizens from their governments through the earlier drive of privatisation of public goods.

The crisis of 2008/2009 did not help in this respect. A forceful, co-ordinated response of countries at the G20 level to avoid the global economic disaster seemed to indicate the return of the state as the most powerful potential actor in steering markets and economies. Despite the nearly unanimous call from politicians and citizens for re-establishing a better balance between markets and governments, however, not much has happened in terms of re-establishing the counterbalancing weight of proactive states. Instead, equity among citizens deteriorated further, unemployment rose and stays at unprecedented levels in many OECD countries, both in aggregate and structural terms.

Citizens are witnessing this lack of effective governance, contributing to a further loss of trust in governments meeting their part of the social contract. According to a nationwide poll carried out in the United Kingdom by IPSOS MORI (in 2011), just one person in six — 17 per cent — professed to trust government ministers. According to the same survey, doctors are the most trusted profession — politicians the least trusted.

Against this background, two tendencies could be particularly important when governments review the potential and constraints for engagement initiatives. On the one hand, the tendency of greater individualism in society is reducing the scope and impact of organised collective action and the search for shared public interest. Individual interests are replacing collective interests as driving forces for change. Evidence is increasing to suggest that when a citizen's self-interest is concerned, they are less likely to engage in pro-social behaviour. Growing inequality introduces another divide: between those who can afford or even benefit from less government and those who need more government urgently because of the economic and social stress of unemployment, age, illness or indebtedness. On the other hand, the question may be raised whether the powerful emergence of civil society is the response of citizens to organise themselves — and an indication of a breakdown in the traditional ways that representative democracy is practiced.

So, how are citizens kept close to governments in light of a continuing modification of the social contract? Should governments put the emphasis in their engagement initiatives on mobilising civil society rather than citizens? In this case, how is this achieved while avoiding the pitfalls of lack of representativeness and the dominance of vested, often one-issue driven interests? How is the civil society model to be reconciled with representative parliamentary systems? How does one exercise leadership in the pursuit of the public interest, which remains the only approach when it comes to climate change, for example?

3. Fiscal consolidation: Co-production as exit strategy for public service delivery?

Fiscal pressures to reduce operating expenditures and to cut program spending are a reality in the majority of OECD countries. Budgetary constraints impose increased transparency in the way governments use public funds. They create momentum for innovative solutions and a rethinking of traditional forms of service delivery, which could, in principle, give citizens more control of their lives. Certain innovations push the boundaries of public service provisions to citizens by defining new forms of public involvement, as documented in the OECD's publication *Together for Better Public Services: Partnering with citizens and civil society.*[4]

The rethinking of traditional public service delivery in a new socio-economic environment transforms the relationship between service users and providers, enabling user control and ownership. While still at a developmental stage in many areas of public service delivery, co-production has started to be mainstreamed in health and social care.

Important challenges, however, exist: quantification of the potential savings; assessment of unintended consequences whereby costs and accountability are shifted onto users and citizens; management capacity at the local level, where most public services would be 'co-produced'; consequences for accountability of policy-makers and risk management in the case of failures of co-production. These are just some of the issues that require intensive analysis and exchange of experiences to test the reality of a new model, which, in principle, could bring governments and citizens closer together, while respecting their mutual responsibilities.

One of the important requirements for a successful new foundation of the government–citizen relationship would be to dispel the suspicion that calls for greater citizen involvement are not driven by the desire to enhance participation, innovation and democracy, but, rather, simply reflects the reality of reduced public resource availability. Nor the even worse belief that co-production is an expression of the belief in the benefits of reducing the state as an objective (of ideology) in itself.

A recent survey by the OECD is not encouraging: the demand for partnerships is predominantly coming from within governments, while citizens and service users are less interested in those sorts of arrangements (Figure 3).

---

4   OECD. 2011. *Together for Better Public Service: Partnering with citizens and civil society*. Paris.

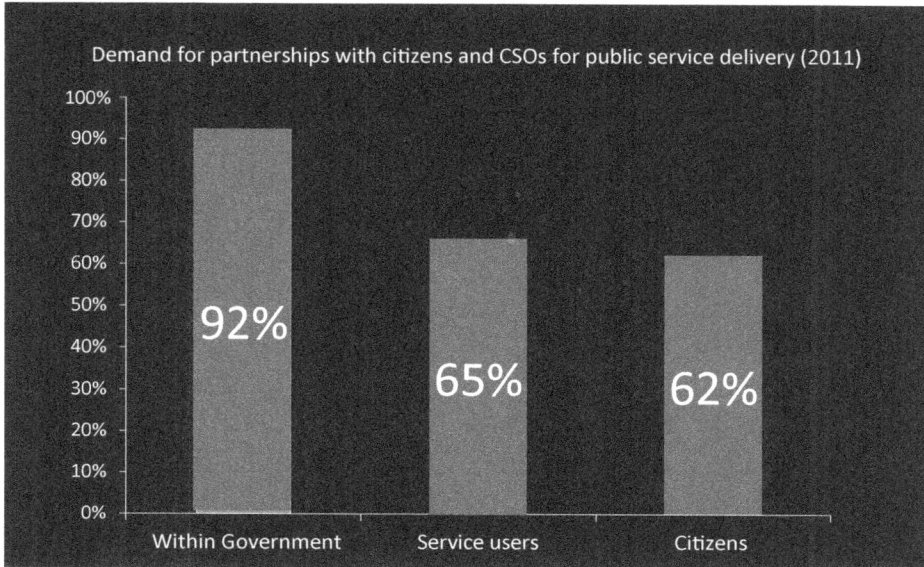

Figure 3: Demand for partnerships with citizens and CSOs for public service delivery (2011)

Source: *Together for Better Public Services–Partnering with Citizens and Civil Societies.*

There is an unfortunate precedent of a misalignment between government and citizen expectations. The quick and firm actions by governments to re-establish confidence, maintain capacity and boost their economies in 2008/2009 were mostly done with very limited or no consultation with citizens, leading to a sense of frustration in not having being invited to decisions that affect the interests of citizens for many years to come. This lack of opportunity for participation — a situation which was felt even by many parliamentarians — may partly explain contemporary resistance to the fiscal consolidation plans of governments. Today, citizens are not fully informed, they do not see the consequences and they do not endorse policy decisions. Essentially, they do not want to be close to their government because their government is not close to them.

Conclusions

Policy-makers in OECD countries and beyond broadly believe that facilitating participation of citizens might enhance democratic engagement, build trust in government and harness productive forms of responsibility, including in the delivery of public services. While the intrinsic value of participation is beyond doubt, the business case is still to be made. More work, and more opportunities for the exchange of practical experience is required.

If governments want to intensify their call on citizens' engagement, it is advisable that they take into account some of the more recent developments which affect the relationship between citizens and governments, in particular the demonstrated importance of social media in the 'awakening' of societies, the erosion of the social contract and the impact of fiscal consolidation measures.

Such broader approaches would put the review of citizen engagement into a wider perspective. Ensuring the re-engagement of governments and citizens requires:

- Better assessment of where the demand for engagement comes from and under which conditions citizens are ready to engage.

- Thinking more thoroughly about the objectives to be achieved from a strong relationship with citizens: for example, how is participation balanced with efficiency, and participation with equity? And how can participation bring innovation to government?

- Reviewing of the institutional structures of government. Does strengthening the dialogue with civil society, for instance, lead to the weakening of parliaments? How is a balance found in this tri-lateral relationship? And how could fiscal institutions, such as fiscal councils or parliamentary budget offices, which are being set up in many OECD countries (including Australia), be helpful in this respect?

- Assessment of the current approach to reforms of the public sector, including the new public management reform paradigm. Have the 'technical' management improvements of the 'new public management' — efficiency rather than effectiveness; technocratic virtues rather than those of build, communicate and implement — run their course, at least at the conceptual level, even if improvements in implementation can still be made?

The discussion of the relationship between citizens and governments will continue, especially in times of serious economic, social and environmental challenges. Many, more fundamental, reflections are being launched about the appropriate model of societies and the role of the state in the 21st century. Has the time of a new governance reform come?

Part II. Drivers for Change: Innovations in citizen-centric governance

5. Engaging Citizens in Policy Innovation: Benefiting public policy from the design inputs of citizens and stakeholders as 'experts'

Christian Bason

In this chapter I will clarify various ways of engaging with citizens and involving them in the processes of policy-making. I would also like to encourage us, as policy actors, to be more conscious about using citizen engagement to reorient what we do to better meet citizens' expectations as well as capture the benefits from inputs of other important actors and stakeholders. The perspective I bring to this contribution is to ask: how can we really engage citizens to *drive innovation* in policies and services, and *help us to produce better* outcomes.

As an important backdrop to our discussion, we need to be aware of the financial crisis affecting governments around the globe. It's a 'perfect storm' involving a toxic mix of financial pressures that are driven by multiple winds of change, with the impacts stemming from demographic change, and from the rising cost of new technologies. Governments are still expected to solve tough social issues and deliver services in this context, while meeting the rising expectations of citizens over the quality of delivery. So, for instance, with demographic changes and ageing we are seeing particular sectors, like the healthcare sector and the social services sector, undergoing massive pressures and transformations across the Organisation for Economic Co-operation and Development (OECD) countries.

Improving meals at the Hvidovre hospital

Let me begin by highlighting what citizen-centric innovation can really mean with an example from the Danish health sector, where a hospital produced significant innovations to the patient experience. At the Hvidovre hospital — a major hospital serving the Copenhagen region — the hospital kitchen serves both the hospital staff and the patients. A few years back, the head chef, Michael Allerup, was irritated because he could see that much of the food his kitchen was producing ended up in waste containers, situated right outside the kitchen window. Patients were not eating what he was producing, there was massive waste and, as a professional chef, this left him dissatisfied.

To deal with the situation, he sought expert help and invited a private sector gourmet chef, Rasmus Bo Bojesen, to offer professional advice. Bojesen was well known for his pastry and ability to deliver excellent food to large groups of people in a professional way. And so began an innovative collaboration between the private sector gourmet chef and the hospital chef. Bojeson began by checking in to the hospital personally, posing as a patient, in a hospital bed, so as to experience for himself what patients experienced every day in terms of the food service. He reviewed the service as a citizen who was knowledgeable about food.

What he saw were poorly presented meals, served at the convenience of management. He realised that the food itself probably wasn't that bad, but it did not look appetising or attractive. He also realised that, the hospital kitchen's service of meals at fixed times of the day, with the same size portions, did not necessarily fit with what patients felt like eating, particularly after an operation, or when they were awake at strange hours of the day.

In short, he experienced for himself the challenges inherent in the existing meal service, and came up with a number of potential solutions, in collaboration with the hospital chef. They introduced a restaurant style menu that allowed clients to select what they wanted, introduced smaller meals for people with limited appetites, due either to age or health, and they used organic and fresh food, and made sure that patients could order meals at any time of the day.

Now, the food at the Hvidovre hospital is inviting and appetising. Of course it's wonderful to be able to prepare better food, and provide the catering service in a way that is tailored to the needs of individual. Certainly, the 'service experience' for patients was dramatically improved, but, more interestingly, under the new arrangements the production of the hospital's food cost 30 per cent less than before, mainly because of less food waste. By catering on and to demand, patients eat the good food that the kitchen produces according to requirements.

That, however, wasn't end of the innovation. Bojesen thought to himself: 'well, we're in a hospital, and I'm wondering whether this food is not also making people more healthy?' In response, he began another process of collaboration with one of the resident doctors to measure whether the better quality food had any impact on patient recovery and the average length of stay at the hospital, and it turned out that it did. It reduced the average amount of stay by approximately one full day. As one would imagine, to be able to make such an average reduction in the length of stay represents a massive saving for the hospital.

This story illustrates some of the value that can come from redesigning services or policies around the citizen experience. In the case of Hvidovre hospital, productivity was increased by savings in catering costs and the reduction in the length of hospital stays; there was a better service experience for citizens, which is what the public expects from a hospital in a wealthy country like Denmark; and, there were also better outcomes in terms of improving health. Clearly, even relatively simple innovations can lead to harvesting benefits in the longer term — a win-win-win situation.

This project was not primarily motivated by notions of democratic participation, or by the agenda of 'patient rights', but simply by redesigning services to suit client needs. The project produced multiple types of value and impacted on multiple bottom lines. This is the real challenge of public sector innovation: to add value across multiple dimensions — not just productivity, but also the service experience — as well as in measurable outcomes. And the interesting point is that, if we start from the citizen's perspective and understand how they experience what we're doing to or for them, these can become the triggers by which we can start to contemplate the generation of value across multiple dimensions.

So, in considering these ideas of citizen-centric governance, citizen-centred innovation, or user-driven innovation, and all the other ways of expressing such initiatives, there seems to be a consensus around the globe that we know there is real value to harvest, and we can produce new value by engaging citizens in new ways. This raises the questions, then, of *how do we do it*, and what are the *best ways of achieving it*? These are the two questions I want to explore in the remainder of this chapter.

Incubating innovation: Denmark's MindLab venture

The agency I lead, MindLab, is focused on these questions while concentrating exclusively on the public sector. MindLab is an active collaboration between three Danish government ministries, businesses and citizens aimed at the co-creation of new public policy and public services.[1] We think of ourselves as a 'citizen-centred innovation' in our own right. MindLab, which has existed for close to 10 years, was originally established by a senior executive of the business ministry, and sponsored by the permanent secretary at that time. When I joined about five years ago, we redesigned and expanded MindLab, adding a research dimension and embedding MindLab in the top management of government.

---

1   MindLab is part of the ministry of business and growth, the ministry of taxation and the ministry of employment. The story of MindLab has been recorded in an online article in the monthly newsletter, *Monocle* (see 'North Stars', 44, June 2011, pp. 121–24). My recent book, *Leading Public Sector Innovation: Co-creating for a better society* (Polity Press, London, 2010), expands on many of the points raised here.

Over the years, MindLab has shifted from its early orientation around the laboratory idea — using a physical space to be creative, to discover, innovate and experiment — to being more about facilitating citizen-centric innovation, more research-oriented, and more about cross-cutting policy issues involving our departments, other levels of government (such as local municipalities) and the community. Our three departments of business and growth, employment, and taxation, share a lot of common policy challenges around, for example, administrative burdens, and engaging with citizens when it makes sense to involve them.

At MindLab we have a specialised staff of 15, consisting of anthropologists, designers, ethnographers, and a few people from the public sector or with a public servant background. We are located within the ministry of business and growth, in a physical space that serves as a platform for collaboration, where public servants work together with us, and with citizens and experts, in a co-creative fashion. We see our role being *not* to come up with bright ideas on behalf of our colleagues, who are public servants like us, but, instead, we facilitate processes and support and help them to create their own better ideas.

The key point I want to make about citizen-centred innovation and involving citizens in better policy design is the importance of finding better ideas that will have a chance of working for the users, and for the policy providers who usually want to invest their time and efforts in policies that work in practice. Being citizen-focused also means that we need to involve public and private sector employees who are not only a good source of ideas, but who will be responsible mainly for overseeing implementation. When we start new projects we ask our colleagues: is this something that you hope will work, or are you just doing it to satisfy the minister or media, or simply to say that you've done it? We ,say if you want to do something that works for people, then you probably need to think about involving them from the outset.

Co-creation of policy through 'professional empathy'

The concept I call 'co-creation' represents a particular take on involving citizens from the start. It's a broad involvement and a holistic one, addressing the question of how we fit citizen engagement into all the dialogues and deliberations we have when we craft new policies. My argument would be that we have to locate the citizens' own reality more centrally in our policy processes, together with our knowledge about citizen expectations and behaviours — in short, we have to capture the citizens' lives. The main message I wish to convey is that we need to get closer to citizens' lives to understand how they do things, to then be able to radically redesign our services. Of course, many other things will be going on in such policy processes — information gathering, costing and consultations, for example, and I am not saying we should replace or abandon everything that we usually do. But, we should add co-creation as something that is important and, potentially, helpful.

I will make three points about co-creation, and this is the essence of the remainder of my chapter. First of all, we need to be involving a wider variety of people in policy design — and I will return to what I mean by that shortly. Second, we need to understand more specifically how people live their lives, what their real experiences are in concrete and qualitative ways — this is a new mode of knowledge that I call 'professional empathy'. And, finally, we should use or orchestrate different kinds of policy creation, or 'service creation processes', inspired by what the best designers do and how designers work in practice.

Encompassing a broader scope of people is about involving more people sooner, early in the policy or service development phase, and about public organisations doing it consciously.

To give a second example, when we were asked to orchestrate a policy process exploring clean environmental technologies and involving six different Danish government departments, including climate change, energy, environment and foreign affairs, we invited the famous Danish–Icelandic artist, Olafur Eliasson, who had done a lot of work about climate change with private companies like BMW, to give a presentation to this group of about 20 senior public servants. Some selected private businesses that were at the forefront of clean technologies, and at the forefront of developing new solutions to climate change, were also invited to attend Eliasson's presentation. The intention was to bring together these different officials from different departments with other types of actors such as artists, business representatives and citizens to gain a common understanding of the multiple challenges we faced. We wanted to facilitate a process of understanding to enable us to craft a business strategy that could both help build Danish commercial success in the field of clean technology and also address climate change.

When Eliasson spoke to this group at a workshop at MindLab, the artist said something along the lines that: 'you know what art can bring to the policy process is a focus on precision, about actually being elitist and very precise about how you want to develop policies; it's about relationships between what you develop as an artist and the observer or the user'. In the case of Eliasson's own artwork, such as his famous artificial sun exhibited at the Tate Modern gallery in London, he is concerned with the interactions with his end users, and this was the key point that the officials took from his presentation. It became a common point of reference across the various silos of government, and it inspired the officials who would be responsible for the process of developing a profitable clean technology sector. The learning experience came about because we chose to involve a wider variety of people in the deliberative process — even unlikely candidates such as, in this case, an artist.

So, most importantly, 'people' are both citizens and end users, but they are certainly also system actors. Often, when we craft new policy services, we don't involve even our own work colleagues as much as we should, or we do it too late for them to understand what's going on or for them to make a meaningful contribution. What I am arguing here is that we should think explicitly about who needs to be involved to bring knowledge and inspiration, and insightful contributions to bear on the process. And, of course, that could potentially be a wide variety of actors, who may not themselves see the connection. The art of the policy facilitator is to find ways of achieving involvement through workshops, interviews, and various types of collaboration that are meaningful to the participants and helpful to the process.

It is true that some of our co-design methods may not suit every citizen, each of whom has different levels of personal capacity. At MindLab we reach citizens or businesses in many different ways, but the important part is to make a strategic selection, and make a reasonable and informed choice about who we want to engage with and how we want to engage with them. Usually we are engaged in onsite fieldwork, which involves going into people's homes or their businesses. We try to capture the range of experiences people have with existing services. Also, to establish a clear picture, we use what we call 'cultural probing', in which we provide people with materials, notebooks, or cameras so that they can document their daily lives or practices and, in doing so, become our informants in a more active way. More formally, we invite participants from different backgrounds and competencies to our workshops and conversations.

You might say, however, that this sounds like a lot of unnecessary work and, of course, it is extra work. But it is all about qualifying policy and gaining inspiration, gaining knowledge from experiences, trying to broker a common understanding of *what the problem really is* that you are attempting to address. And I would say the crucial task for managers is to orchestrate the process in ways where we don't involve everyone all the time, but we do it in ways that are meaningful and sensible. The key point I want to make here is that end user citizens and businesses need to be at the heart of that process, while others can make valuable contributions too.

This new mode of policy knowledge, the so-called 'professional empathy', is about the systematic ability for a public organisation, or any organisation, to experience what citizens experience, just as the gourmet chef Bojesen did at the Hvidovre hospital, jumping into the hospital bed and experiencing for himself what it felt like personally to receive the food service. And, of course, there are many ways of involving citizens. We can involve citizens in understanding the present or the past through quantitative surveys, or through more qualitative research; we can also engage with citizens to craft a new future. And we need to do both in order to anchor our innovation efforts in citizens' experience and in reality.

Focusing on qualitative citizen engagement in policy creation processes

Usually, when policy-makers seek input from citizens in policy processes they spend most of their time on quantitative metrics and surveys. These are valuable inputs oriented towards the responsive-end of the policy spectrum, telling us about citizen reactions, but they don't tell us anything about what to change. They may tell us something about how big the problem is, but not specifically what needs to be changed to alleviate the problem. So we need to go much deeper and move more toward qualitative inputs in order to drive innovation. Accordingly, at MindLab we concentrate on the qualitative ways of understanding citizens' experiences — trying to get to the designer-end of the spectrum and exploring other types of engagement. In running design-driven workshops, we are seeking ways to co-create policy from the outset that will involve quality delivery through co-operation and mutual forms of collaboration.

A few further examples will illustrate the point of getting up close and qualitative with citizens. In Denmark, we have come a long way in understanding administrative burdens on businesses — burdens that waste time and place additional costs on business. The government has pledged to reduce such administrative burdens as part of creating a pro-business, pro-innovation environment. Rules, regulations and government requirements have to be experienced as sensible and meaningful to business, otherwise they are counterproductive. To highlight such dilemmas, we often send colleagues into the field with video cameras to record the experiences of stakeholders, and show what it feels like to be on the receiving-end of government bureaucracy and red tape. To this end, we have filmed Danish farmers trying to negotiate their way through the Danish bureaucracy and its complicated administrative burdens. When filming and interviewing, we try to understand what the triggers are that irritate or annoy, or seem meaningless to business, and we try to understand how they feel as actors within the system.

Another example would be when we questioned citizens who had serious work injuries about what it felt like to be receiving the service package from the Danish board of industrial injuries — a public agency intent on being an efficient case manager. We conducted in-depth, qualitative interviews with only a few citizens, but, significantly, we stayed with these citizens in their homes to feel what it was really like to be treated as an injured worker by the system. In their homes they could show us all the files, the 25 different letters, all the processing and insurance papers they had accumulated, and all of the complicated administrative work that goes into settling a work injury case. And what we found when we examined their unfortunate experiences through their own eyes, was that the way the system works often makes people more sick than they are already. This insight was fundamental for the operations of the industrial injury agency. It took the findings seriously, and began working in many different ways to make the outcome of undergoing a work injury case a more meaningful and positive experience for the citizen.

Obviously, staff working for the agency did not go to work every day trying to make people more sick — and, in fact, many hope that they are doing a good job — but our qualitative research exposed many problems in the system and showed that the agency has the potential to significantly better its performance so as to improve the experience for those injured. The agency is now trying to redesign its policies around the citizen experience, and is trying to leverage the funding mechanisms — including the private insurers — to invest more in the citizens' abilities, helping them get back on their feet, paying off their mortgages and ultimately finding a job again. Being creative is also about rethinking funding incentives and opportunities to use resources differently to enhance outcomes.

Another case in which MindLab qualitatively studied citizens' experiences was when we explored why young Danish citizens do not use online digital tax services. The Danish tax ministry reported statistics that showed the age group in Denmark that was *least* likely to use online digital tax services were people under 30. The ministry could produce the figures and the statistics, but they did not understand why the most digitally aware generation in Denmark were not using the services. So, we interviewed Dennis, a 23-year-old apprentice who had just got his first job. We asked him why he, and young citizens like him, did not use online processing for his tax affairs. And, in the course of our interview, we discovered that of course Dennis has a computer, uses it, and even has broadband. But he does not 'get the tax language', and nor does he understand the logic of the site developed by the tax ministry. For example, he is uncertain of the process required of him to alert the system when he receives a higher salary from his emplyer. To him therefore, it makes more sense to get in his car and drive the 23 kilometres to the local municipal office where he can have his tax affairs done manually by the nice staff member there. This is costly and contrary to the digitisation efforts of the tax ministry.

We explored what it would take to get Dennis to be able to complete a transaction online. We began by observing how he used a computer and what understanding he had of the online sites he visited. Armed with this information, the tax ministry is now beginning a major re-conceptualisation process to try to find a way of redesigning the interface and facilitating interaction between young people, or any citizen for that matter, and the tax system.

Finally, we recently helped five Danish ministries understand what it would feel like to be an immigrant worker entering the country hoping for work. In this case we chose, amongst others, a highly qualified Indian engineer who arrived in Denmark and tried to find a job, start a new life and manage a family in an unfamiliar country. We started by interviewing eight to 10 individuals in similar circumstances to help share their experiences since their arrival in Denmark, and especially with the Danish public services. Their stories were of disempowerment, being passed from agency to agency, unable to comprehend the systems, often being left waiting, and suffering language problems. The experience for the immigrant family was not discernible to the five ministries individually, but we managed to get a common understanding across to these agencies of what might need to be improved for such new residents.

Design-inspired processes, visualisation and mapping

You may well be asking yourself: if we are just asking citizens what they want, they will simply want more from us. Also, if we are using qualitative inputs, it is not genuinely representative to just interview six, eight or 10 people. And, of course, it isn't. But there is enormous value in going deeper with a limited number of sources and obtaining concrete information about their experiences. It turns out that if we interview eight or 10 people, or even fewer, about a certain service experience, similar patterns emerge very quickly. And, even though the interviewees may be of different gender, age, and come from different locations, we often find surprisingly coherent patterns of experience that can then drive policy and service design. Hence, I would argue that it's not about being quantitative and statistically representative, rather, it's about harvesting insights that can drive ideation and creation, which is the third component of what I refer to as co-creation.

So far, I have discussed citizen involvement, using expertise and knowledge and gaining inspiration, and about understanding the qualitative experience — but what about creation and the creative process? This is a different kind of process, which might be called 'rehearsing the future' — a term coined by the *Danmarks Designskole* (Danish Design School) in Copenhagen. It involves using a design-inspired process to drive the creation of policy and service.

There are two dimensions of design as a practice. The first is design as a product-related discipline, establishing or following the conventions when we are styling fashion or new cars, using graphic design, or designing gadgets or mobile phones. The second dimension of design is far broader in scope than the first and it consists of creating desirable futures. So, designing becomes the practice of creating new futures, and that can involve public services, and it can certainly be applied to systems, organisations and strategies.

To adopt the second meaning of design requires a new set of attitudes and a way of seeing the world, which is not only analytical (something governments are usually good at), but it also emphasises the value of synthesis, looks more holistically at solutions, and looks at what works for people. My argument is that to do this we need to put things together, to apply the mindset of synthesis and develop coherent, meaningful services for people. We need to think about prototyping ideas and innovations — thinking through doing — getting practical and concrete about things. We need to be serious about design not just as an attitude or approach to the world but as a creative process of design action.

Design action is about challenging assumptions — something we rarely do well as public servants. We often take for granted the overall policy framework, or the suggestions we receive from ministers or parliament. And we should be loyal servants, but being a loyal servant can also be about questioning underlying assumptions and, sometimes, about helping reframe what the true problem is. As I mentioned earlier, by getting close to citizens, it is sometimes possible to reframe the fundamental problem. For instance, in the case of the injured workers, the problem was not how do we run an efficient case management process, rather, the problem was that we were making the administrative process meaningless to people; we were making them sicker than they already were, and we were not helping them return to the labour market, and get their lives back on track.

The best designers are certainly concerned with how real people — customers, citizens, users, or whatever — engage with solutions, services, products, artefacts, and systems. In designing policy or services, it is necessary to have the human dimension foremost. We have to understand what drives behaviour and what behaviours are apparent or likely to emerge, what drives motivation and, ultimately, what drives outcomes. That is, in many ways, a fundamental design discipline.

Experimental design and prototyping are ways of testing out solutions, not as pilots to gauge risk, but as very early first drafts that are even built to fail. We may use prototypes consciously to fail, to learn rapidly, and then intuitively try something different, and then move forward. Because it's an experimental process, however, it requires public servants to be willing to create and test rough drafts. Citizens need to be given the opportunity to say what works in a particular context. This is the tougher creative challenge; we are just trying stuff out to see what works. And that is what we need to do if we want to get policy and services right.

Finally, using visual tools to enable conversations with citizens is also a useful way of obtaining concrete insight into the experiences of citizens. One exercise that we have tried is getting high school students to engage in a conversation about their understanding of money matters, personal finances and tax issues. We wanted a dialogue, so we used a visual tool like a target to help the students prioritise what was most important to them, to assemble all the ideas that we had generated with them into some structure, and into a rough prioritisation.

Visual tools, graphic design and other design tools can help keep the conversation more concrete, more specific, and more tangible about what is needed. At times, we also use role playing exercises and, in this case, we worked with several agencies to conduct a small-scale role playing exercise to negotiate financial transactions and show who might be involved in the service design processes. We gave participants an idea of what a new policy would look and feel like for each of the various actors involved. That is really what designing services can be about — making them visual and concrete.

From the citizen's perspective, we can also use 'service journey mapping' as a way of visualising the pathway of the citizen through the system by capturing all the different interactions they are likely to encounter. So, for instance, an injured Danish worker may experience 'points of pain' in the system at which the system makes no sense to him/her, and this leads to confusion and frustration. And, given the bulk of correspondence some of these individuals have received from the agency, their frustration is not as a result of being uninformed. The problem is that they are probably over-informed and the system and its language does not make sense.

Service journey mapping is a way of visualising services from the vantage point of the citizens, and then using these maps as a driver of common understanding when, for example, various public agencies need to coordinate or collaborate to improve service quality. Agencies can use such mappings to assess what resources there are across the delivery chain, to re-evaluate resource deployment to improve experiences and to consider which can be used more effectively to co-produce a new service scenario. The capacity to have such a citizen-centric overview of the system level is critical in assessing the potential for processes of co-creation and system redesign.

Conclusion: Citizens as experts in their own lives

Using design as a driver in innovation in government is not something that only MindLab is doing. In Australia, the Australian Centre for Social Innovation is using design approaches in its efforts in Adelaide, South Australia. In Finland, the Helsinki Design Lab is working with government officials to bring design — and 'strategic design', as they call it — into government. In France, the so-called 27th Region works with the French regions to redesign regional policies. And, in the United Kingdom, there are a number of consultancies and not-for-profit organisations that are working with design approaches to help craft new government services.

So, the emphasis on design is not something that is novel to Denmark. We are seeing it grow as a discipline and being applied in new ways in social services and in policy. Maybe what we are witnessing in many parts of the globe is the beginning of design being used as a major approach or tool in crafting policies.

Naturally, other tricky issues are raised when we adopt these design principles, such as those concerning relative resourcing, whom to consult, and managing heightened expectations once the design process is underway. From my experience, most people understand that they are not in the process to make decisions, but that they are involved to help qualify decisions that will be made by others who can bring other considerations to bear on the issues. The key point about citizen engagement is that we involve citizens, like the injured workers or the students mentioned earlier, to interrogate them as experts in what they are experts in, which is their own lives. That is the key reason for the sort of co-design or co-creative approaches we are advocating.

To conclude, the three principles of co-creation I have stressed are: getting close-up to citizens and end users, and understanding their concrete experiences; 'zooming out' to the system level to understand what better outcomes we can co-create and how we can deliver them; and, shifting our narrow thinking about service delivery to thinking synoptically about what are the entire set or resources — citizen resources, businesses, and others in society, which can be better utilised to help create better outcomes.

The management challenge today is to recognise that these insights about how citizens experience services can be very powerful, and will need to be accepted by public organisations. The tough part now will be to accept the organisational consequences and the necessary changes to systems, processes, behaviours, and attitudes within the system so as to accommodate the insights and the new solutions we discover. That is the challenge — the change management task. I might even go so far as to say that it calls for change *leadership*. But that's a different story.

6. Engaging Citizens in Co-producing Service Outcomes

John Alford

Much of this volume concerns the involvement of citizens in deciding *what* to do or *how* to do it, principally through what I call the 'co's' — consultation, co-deliberation and co-design. The assumption is that a particular service will be delivered to citizens by government. Co-production, the subject of this chapter, takes the process further by having citizens take part in *producing* the service. This is a fundamental difference, and it is gaining popularity among governments around the world. On balance, I think that this is a good thing.

I find, however, that alongside this flourishing interest in the idea of co-production exist many myths; each of the key issues in co-production has its own misconception to shadow it. In this chapter I will address both the issues and the misconceptions that surround co-production in tandem. The issues to be addressed offer a road map of what I shall talk about, focusing on the following five key questions: What is co-production? What do we mean by citizens? How do we identify potential co-producers? When should co-production be utilised? How can co-production be elicited from citizens? Each of these questions is shadowed by a misconception, which I will address later in the chapter.

What is co-production? The popular understanding of this concept is that it concerns joint deliberation or consultation — in other words, citizens being involved in deciding what to do or how to do something as well as producing it. This is a loose usage of the term, however, leading to its indiscriminate employment. The word production is not used to include deciding what to do, so why use the word co-production to include co-deciding what to do? Co-production is about doing something, not about deciding what to do. That is not to say that co-decision is not important. But it is something different from co-production. Nor is it to say that, when co-productive processes are taking place, there isn't a lot of co-deliberation happening alongside it. What I want to do is to analytically distinguish co-production as a term.

There are a number of considerations in defining the term. When there is a service to be provided, there are three possible scenarios: it could be provided by a government organisation acting alone, by an external party acting alone, or, it could be achieved jointly between them. The other thing that marks the distinction between deciding what to do and actually doing it is that, strictly speaking, co-production is the process of something being undertaken jointly by a government organisation and an external party.

It's never that simple, however. There are some activities, like planning and design, for example, with their emphasis on the activity that is to be co-produced, which lie in a grey area between co-production and co-decision. Examples of such crossover can be found in architecture or town planning.

Further than that, there are activities undertaken by private parties — be they companies, individuals or whatever — that have no apparent connection with government. Their involvement arises because of government influence, and I think we need to acknowledge this phenomenon — what I call 'nudged production' or 'self-service', following Richard Thaler and Cass Sunstein (2008). An example of this technique is the way in which a driver will slow down at an intersection because of the presence of a roundabout. To an extent, the driver is being nudged by the government to slow down, thereby contributing to the public purpose of reducing the road toll.

In other words, co-production is not only something that is undertaken jointly, but also things that are prompted by some action, behaviour or incentive provided by a government agency. This can include planning and design, but, certainly, the real focus is on actually doing it.

The second term to define is *citizen*. What do we mean by this? There can be a failure to distinguish between different faces of a citizen — a point that is raised by Lynelle Briggs (Chapter 7). It is important to acknowledge that citizens are, first and foremost, always part of the collective 'we' who: contribute to determining what government should do through all the processes of democracy enjoyed in Australia, benefit from the public value that governments create and, who have various rights and responsibilities associated with both of those things.

Above all, therefore, we are all citizens, but I want to argue that we have multiple other roles in which we can function as co-producers. Firstly, we are also clients: we can be both a citizen and a client. As citizens we interact with government in terms of public value while, as clients, we interact with services that might provide some private value. In fact, often our enjoyment of the private value contributes to public value in the process — when school pupils get an education, for example, that is good for them as individuals in their life prospects, but it's also good for the wider society that citizens are literate, numerate and knowledgeable in the myriad ways provided by an education.

Students at state school are examples of beneficiary clients — people who receive services but don't pay money for them, even though they are receiving what we might call 'private value'. A second group are what we might call 'obligatees' or 'regulatees' — that is, people who are subjected to obligations by government agencies. This also affects their private value, often negatively, and we impose obligations on people on behalf of the society at large, through which the individual is disadvantaged for the sake of the public at large. These are different kinds of interactions than those between the government and the collective citizenry.

In fact, co-production can give an additional, vital reason for governments to pay attention to their clients. In their 1992 book, *Reinventing Government: How the Entrepreneurial Spirit is Transforming the Public Sector*, David Osborne and Ted Gaebler argue that government organisations are hopeless at client service because they don't get any money from their clients, and therefore have no incentive to provide good service. I would argue there is another incentive: while clients don't contribute money, they can contribute co-productive effort if the relationship is properly managed. Clients are more likely to do that if government agencies try to understand what it is that they want, and try to give it to them — which is essentially client focus.

Citizens can also be people who make voluntary contributions, outside of service encounters with government. Formal volunteering involves working for a government department or a not-for-profit or community organisation — examples include the Country Fire Service or Meals on Wheels. But volunteering may also involve random acts of sociability and helpfulness in the community. These acts contribute something to the community as a whole, even if they are not organised through the formal channels of government or non-profit community organisations.

When I refer to citizens in this chapter, therefore, I exclusively refer to beneficiary clients, obligatees-regulatees and volunteers.

This leads me to the next question: *how do we identify potential co-producers?* The answer to this question provides the basis for challenging another misconception about co-production which, with due deference to Eliza Doolittle and the play *My Fair Lady*, I call the 'wouldn't it be loverly' misconception. This describes the view that co-production is a new thing which would be nice to have. In fact, my research shows that in many, and probably most areas of public sector work, co-production is already an established reality.

Let me explain by way of an example. Think of a fire brigade in output terms: that its purpose is to put out fires quickly and efficiently. This is the general view we have of the work of fire brigades. But the process of putting out a fire is, in fact, far more complex. To illustrate this point, imagine the various processes at work, from when a house catches fire. Before the blaze can be put out, a core 'production process' must take place. First 000 might be called, following which a dispatcher sends a fire truck, which speeds to the fire; the fire is then hosed with water.

What this highlights is a *core* production process. Once 000 has been called, most of the work is done internally by the fire brigade; thus we're talking so far about the *internal* production of desired outputs. But, when you start to think about the work of a fire brigade, it becomes clear that these internal processes rely on processes performed by external parties, which I call co-productive contributions. For a start, external parties like neighbours or property owners and occupants ring 000 — or more generally. to install smoke alarms. The functioning of 000, and of the fire despatcher, relies on maintenance contractors keeping telecoms up to date. Next the fire engine needs to be ready to go, which relies on regular servicing by mechanics. For the fire engine to speed to the fire, the streets need to be accessible, for which the road authorities are responsible. And finally, to hose the fire with water there needs to be a fire hydrant — a responsibility of the relevant water corporation. What we have unearthed, therefore, is that there are two types of contributors to the output of a fire brigade. Firstly, there are the internal contributors — the clients and staff that work inside the fire brigade. But there are also the external co-producers, such as the people who make slippery poles or keep the roads drivable. A fire brigade relies on contributions of time and effort by external factors.

So far we've only been considering the purpose of a fire brigade framed in *output* terms, but when we go further and frame it in *outcome* terms — namely, to minimise the fire damage to life, property and the environment — we find that co-production is an even bigger part of the picture. What's more, this broader outcome can be achieved in a variety of ways in addition to the output of the fire brigade. Firstly, it is more likely to happen if there is timely evacuation from the burning house — which is, in turn, more likely if the owner or occupant has a fire response plan. A positive outcome is also more likely if the fire occurs but has less impact on the house — something which largely depends on whether the house was built to resist fire (and whether the property owner did the right thing in terms of building requirements), another function of the owners and occupants.

This example shows that, when it comes to the outcome terms of a fire brigade, the property owner or occupant — i.e., the nearest thing the fire brigade has to a client — has to do some work to ensure that the purpose of the brigade is achieved. The potential contributors to the outcome, be they property owners or roads authorities, do more than just call 000 and sit back and wait for the service to be delivered to them; they play an active part in reducing the damage that fires might inflict.

Outcome focus also changes the nature of the work done by the fire brigade itself. Not only are they engaged in delivering their important service of putting out fires, they are also seeking to induce others to contribute to their ultimate purpose of reducing harm from fires; for example, by educating the community on fire safety through school visits and other such endeavours. In addition to this education component, technical advice is provided to building owners and occupiers about ensuring the minimisation of fire damage. They all play a role in contributing to this outcome. So, the fire brigade is in the business not only of delivering services but also of influencing others.

This relates to the 'wouldn't it be loverly syndrome' that I mentioned earlier, because it shows that co-production is not just something that it would be nice to have. In fact, it's already happening in the normal functioning of many public services. My research suggests that most public services entail at least some element of co-production, and I think this resonates with the point Don Kettl (Chapter 3) raises about naming a problem that can't be confined to one organisation when you start to look at it seriously. In a sense we've been co-producing all our lives without knowing it.

This leads to my next question: *when should co-production be utilised?* It also raises what I call the 'exploitation misconception' — that co-production is about government getting citizens to shoulder the cost of service delivery. The answer to the question of when co-production should be utilised depends on the particular characteristics of the case at hand. On one hand co-production is not the answer to all the problems known to humankind. On the other, it's not something to be dismissed out of hand every time it is raised. Instead, whether to utilise co-production depends on the circumstances.

As Kettl points out, there is no one-size-fits-all use for co-production; the context determines its suitability. Sometimes co-production is not an effective tool of government, especially when it is ill thought-out, maybe unnecessary and has not involved a process of meaningful consultation and participation in decision-making by citizens. Such cases usually occur when governments have orchestrated co-production for cosmetic purposes or other superficial reasons. If, however, there is more public value coming from people doing things in a particular way, and those individuals who are doing those things are themselves gaining more value, then the endeavour is worthwhile — a valuable exchange.

What then, are these circumstances? The first of them is what I call *interdependency*, which is where value cannot be created without some contribution from an external party. In other words, the internal process is bound up with the external process. In that situation, the question is not *whether* to co-produce but rather *how* best to utilise the co-production.

Such reforms have been evident in programs for the unemployed, with or without mutual obligation. They involve seeking to get the unemployed to take steps to find work; it can be difficult for an employment agency to get someone into a job unless the unemployed improve their suitability by training, searching for jobs, making a favourable impression on an employer and maintaining that impression (for at least three months, so that they count in the success story statistics). It is also apparent, for example, in health, child protection, conservation and road safety.

The second circumstance is where the services are *substitutable* and value can be achieved by either the organisation or by the external party; that is, they are substitutes for each other. And here the issue is which party can do it better or cheaper? Similarly with the debate over whether or not to outsource a particular service, the question is whether it is delivered more successfully in house, or by an outside provider. This is where the exploitation myth comes in, and where it's also, in my view, refuted. Some advocates of citizen co-production focus on its potential to reduce the size and therefore the costs of government — I think David Cameron's so-called 'Big Society' has a whiff of that about it — that it will be achieved by handing over some of the burden to citizens.

But the weight of the available research indicates that co-production is better for *enhancing value* rather than reducing costs. In other words, for a given level of costs you can get a better outcome, rather than having the same outcome for less cost. I would argue, and I think the research supports this, that the exploitation of citizen co-producers doesn't usually work, and this has to do with the nature of the reasons why citizens co-produce, to which we now turn.

How can co-production be elicited from citizens? This question raises what I call the 'motivation misconception', and there are two distinct, but simplistic, schools of thought on this issue. One school argues that citizens will only co-produce when it's in their self-interest do so — to get monetary reward or avoid sanctions. The other school argues that citizens will co-produce if they are stirred by altruism. But the reasons for citizens engaging in co-production are more complex than either self-interest or altruism. In fact, co-productive behaviours by external parties stem from two factors. One is their *willingness* to co-produce, but the other is their *ability* to do so, and these are in turn prompted, at least partly, by things the organisation does to or for or with them, which I call 'motivators' or 'facilitators.' These can be framed in various ways (John et al. 2011).

Our willingness to co-produce usually stems from a mixture of motivators, and these can be divided into material and non-material factors. The motivators of material self-interest are sanctions — such as punishment, pain, deprivation of liberty, financial loss — or material reward — such as money, health or amenity. While these are important, they are not the sole reasons why people co-produce. Also affecting people's propensity to co-produce are non-material motivations: intrinsic interest, sense of social belonging or desire to avoid disapproval, and identification with the purpose of the organisation or program — or the 'mission alignment' of the external party with the organisation's purpose.

These non-material motivations cannot be reduced simply to altruism. Economists sometimes talk of either self-interest or altruism influencing behaviour, but, in fact, I think these motivations are more complex than that. Consider the following example of a case of mission alignment in which someone joins the military because of national pride. Now, national pride can be a good thing or a bad thing, depending on how it's used, but it is definitely a larger motivator than our own self-interest. The propensity of individuals to enlist in the military is partly a function of how justifiable they think the war is that they're being asked to fight. These non-material motivations interact with material self-interest in various ways to encourage, if not coerce or manipulate, people to co-produce.

The propensity to co-produce is not simply a matter of willingness but also of the individual's ability to do so. Two options arise in situations in which people feel unable to perform a particular task: change the task or change the people. Changing the task might mean simplifying it so as to enable the individual to be more capable of completing it; for example, by introducing a simple, single digit number (000) rather than a multi-digit one. The other approach is to make the citizen more capable of doing a task; for example, through the use fire drills or job-search training.

Eliciting co-production from citizens can only work if it amounts to a value-creating *social* exchange, in which the government receives co-productive effort by citizens and the citizen receives some mix of material and non-material rewards. Both parties should get more than they give. This is a social rather than an economic exchange because it involves diffuse and differed dealings among multiple parties — not immediate quid pro quo transactions among the buyers and sellers in the market. Those who have read the literature on social exchange, or Robert Titmuss' book, *The Gift Relationship* (1970) will be familiar with this.

In short, citizen co-producers are not Pavlovian respondents to carrots and sticks. If they are willing to contribute time and effort to organisational purposes, they do so for their own good reasons, which are only partially influenced by the motivators and facilitators that are offered by government.

In conclusion, co-production is not just a nice idea — it is already embedded in public activities. The question is one of making the best of it, not whether we should do it. Nor is co-production about getting citizens to do work that should be done by government; whether co-production should be used at all depends on the circumstances. And finally, in closing, citizens produce for their own good reasons, which can be only partially influenced.

References

John, P., Cotterill, S., Moseley, A., Richardson, L., Smith, G., Stoker, G., and Wales, C. 2011. *Nudge, Nudge, Think, Think: Using experiments to change civic behaviour.* London: Bloomsbury Academic.

Osborne, D., and Gaebler, T. 1992. *Reinventing Government: How the entrepreneurial spirit is transforming the public sector.* Reading: Addison Wesley.

Thaler, R.H. and Sunstein, C.R. 2008. *Nudge: Improving decisions about health, wealth and happiness.* New Haven: Yale University Press.

Titmuss, R. 1970. *The Gift Relationship.* London: Allen & Unwin.

7. Citizens, Customers, Clients or Unwilling Clients? Different and effective strategies for citizen-centric delivery

Lynelle Briggs

In this chapter I will explore the shift to 'citizen-centred service delivery models' in the Australian Public Service (APS) and touch on some of the associated theories and international developments. In doing so, there are a couple of key questions we need to consider. The first is how are we changing the way we engage with citizens? And secondly, is what we are doing enough? It is also important to consider the key opportunities for, and challenges to, realising truly people-centred services: it is not only necessary to raise the standards of government interactions with the community, but also to radically rethink how some services are designed and delivered.

How are we changing the way we engage with citizens in Australia?

Let me begin by recounting a little of my own recent experiences with service delivery reform. In doing so, I will touch on some of the main drivers for reform, give an idea of the scope of the structural changes underway in the APS in the service delivery arena and highlight some of the things that have been happening in the human services portfolio to enhance community engagement.

As many readers would know, on 1 July 2011, three great APS institutions — Medicare Australia, Centrelink and the Department of Human Services — came together to form one department of state. This milestone creates a new department that will give policy clout to service delivery, with service delivery now being recognised as a valid policy stream in itself. The department is driving a new way of delivering health access services, income support and child support services to the Australian community. That new way is all about:

- merging services so that they are refocussed to deliver better results for people
- having the information and tools to assist Australians in accessing a range of community or other services that might meet their needs

- Australians feeling that they are able to work with the department to devise new services that better meet their needs, share in the design of those services and advise on the best method of delivery of the services to them

- transforming the department's operations electronically and procedurally to provide the basis for all of this to happen.

The merger is a large operation by anyone's standards: 40,000 staff, 550 offices, 170 programs and services, and contacts with just about every Australian each year. The department is the face of the Australian Government in the community; we have an enormous opportunity to deliver change.

The creation of the new department signals one of the most significant changes for the delivery of social and health payments and related services in Australia since the mid 1990s. It is a direct response to the need to put the people we serve at the centre of our work and build our structures around them.

Today, Australians and New Zealanders expect quality services from government, reliable advice from expert service staff and convenient online access. We expect quick, convenient service for straightforward services like pension or Medicare payments or entitlement adjustments, but we want higher level service that delivers results when we are in need or in trouble.

We expect to be treated like individuals with particular needs, to be treated with respect and courtesy, and to be able to trust the public sector to be there when we need it.

In short, Australians expect to see services delivered in ways that work for them. For this reason we devised the catchphrase 'easy, high quality and work for you'[1] — our aim for service delivery reform.

To deliver on this bold reform promise is a huge undertaking and people want to know how to do it. In my opinion, it is necessary to:

- move systematically, thoughtfully and respectfully

- make your vision a priority

- align your people and your stakeholders with the vision and ensure that your people desire the reform

- align values; use what is valued as a base, and build on that. In the public service, making people's lives better is always a good place to start because those core values are a strong part of every public servant

- have a plan; we have a large and complex plan with clear lines of accountability and time scales, which is driven from the top. The plan has a

---

1   This is the catchphrase for service delivery reform throughout the Department of Human Services.

national roll out so, while we are piloting some elements, we are not shirking the responsibility to drive reform nationally and to deliver nationwide

- fix the blockages. At this stage, that is about integrating our systems and processes and making our online systems easy and intuitive for everyone to use; but it has also been about bringing our managers on board with the changes.

But, perhaps above all, active leadership, persistence and determination are critical to successfully undertaking such a transformation. We have focused on senior leadership unity, service leader alignment in the field, and a thousand or so 'transformers' among our staff who are facilitating the change.

This requires us to have at the forefront of our thinking the need to progressively take the portfolio to another place where we could truly put people at the centre of everything we do. With that change, design and delivery of services should become 'outside in', with Australians telling us what they want and need — as opposed to the more traditional, internally driven 'tell you' model — and with new service offers being based on people's life events and local issues rather than the silly procedural requirements of some support programs.[2]

What you told us: Acting on everyday Australians' feedback

So that Australians could tell us what they wanted, the portfolio agencies conducted a series of community forums across the country to gain insight from the people who used our services. This was a first step in our commitment to develop a co-design approach and build mechanisms to more actively engage the people who use our services in designing them as well.

The forums gave us a better understanding of how people experience our services, the obstacles they face and their daily frustrations. It showed the diversity and complexity of circumstances and preferences surrounding people's use of and access to government services.

These forums also identified four common themes in people's expectations of service delivery. Firstly, people said 'make it about me'; as much as possible, they wanted services to be personalised and tailored to their individual needs at different times in their lives. Secondly, they said 'connect me where it counts'; they were looking for better coordinated services that would deliver results for them, easier and quicker access to these services, and services that are linked between different tiers of government. Thirdly, people wanted things to be 'clear

---

2   We are, of course, bound by the legislative and policy-driven requirements of government programs.

and simple'; they were in search of good communication and information, simple processes and forms and intuitive online services and they wanted to deal with staff who understood and had empathy for their circumstances. And, finally, they said 'give me flexibility'. People were looking for easy and appropriate access. This did not necessarily always mean online services, although that is certainly now the preferred channel for most Australians. Some people still prefer face-to-face options, and most people prefer to talk to someone when they are dealing with sensitive or complex situations.

Naturally enough, it's when things get complex that we must really work hard to meet people's expectations. As one participant in the forums described their experience with the portfolio: '… if you just have general process stuff, it's good; the problem is when things fall down. If things get complicated that's when it gets bad'. This quote also highlights the fact that policy officers need to have a much clearer sense of the service delivery implications of their work, because what works logically on paper doesn't always work smoothly on the ground.

Naturally, the four themes that emerged from the forums are interdependent. These themes were the focus of the frustrations participants felt with existing service delivery as well as the bases of their suggestions for improvement. Two of the most important ideas that emerged for improvement were 'personalised service delivery', including a case management approach and 'linked up services', with the idea of a 'one-stop shop'. While these might not be radically new ideas, they do confirm that we were on track with our assumptions about people's expectations.

They also amplify how important it is for people on both sides of the counter to have an understanding of each other. For example, an Indigenous Australian participant said: '… they don't know what's going on in the outside world and we don't know what's going on in the inside. They need to come out to our communities and experience what it's like for us, to live like us and make it real for them. It should be part of their training'.

The then minister for human services, Tanya Plibersek, asserted that policy needed to begin in the real world, stating: 'getting out and seeing firsthand what is happening in communities should be an important part of your jobs as public servants'. And that is exactly the challenge that has been set for the APS through the 2010 *Blueprint for Reform*, which we have met by, for example, hosting ongoing forums, staff dialogues, town hall meetings in partnership with local government in Victoria, and community agency suggestions.

Citizens, customers or clients?

On the question of whether we use the terms 'citizens', 'customers' or 'clients', I don't care much; they are all people to me, but anyone who has even a passing acquaintance with *Ahead of the Game: Blueprint for reform of Australian Government administration* will be aware that it is peppered with references to 'citizens'. One of the primary reforms it identifies is forging a stronger relationship with citizens through better delivery of services and through greater involvement of citizens in their government.

Whether in the market-driven models of former heads of government Ronald Reagan in the United States and Margaret Thatcher in Britain, former UK prime minister Tony Blair's 'third way' or John Howard's former government's market-driven reforms in Australia, one phrase that seemed to gain almost universal currency in the literature and in government circles was 'customer focus'. It was a common theme that governments should adopt more of a private sector approach to dealing with their citizenry.

Governments were responding to the rising expectations of 'consumers', with a model which emphasised choice, competition, contestability and market-testing as ways of achieving efficiencies. 'Customer focus' came to be regarded as an antidote to the widely held notion that a traditional bureaucracy was characterised by red tape, inertia and rule-bound administrators providing one-size-fits-all models of service delivery.

Not everyone, however, accepted the validity of the 'customer' concept in the specific circumstances of the public sector. Many felt that it did not adequately capture the relationship between government organisations and members of the public and served, rather, to devalue the notion of citizenship. Treating the public only as customers, some thought, reduced them to passive recipients of services, rather than active participants, and ignored the fact that many people had no choice other than to deal with government.

John Alford considers 'citizens' to be those who receive 'public value' from government.[3] He makes a distinction between this collective citizenry and a subset of citizens with whom an agency deals at its 'business end', and who receive 'private value'. Alford defines the latter group as 'clients', and he sub-characterises them as 'paying clients', 'beneficiaries' and 'obligatees'. The latter group might also be called unwilling clients, such as prisoners or detainees, who

---

3   John Alford, 'Defining the Clients in the Public Sector: A social exchange perspective', *Public Administration Review*, May/June 2002, volume 62, no 3.

are the recipients of 'services' they don't necessarily want. In his view only the 'paying clients' conform to the private sector market model — one which is primarily based on economic exchange.

Searching for a broader notion of exchange that would better align with the complex relationships between government organisations and the public, Alford turned to social-exchange theory, which extends the concept of exchange beyond economic benefits to include intangible ones, such as the affirmation of social norms. As Terry Moran has put it: '… there are important elements, such as a measure of shared responsibility for the wellbeing of all in our community and the social cohesion it promotes that are not readily tradeable in a market place'.[4]

The social-exchange perspective asserts the importance of encouraging public servants to think about their relationships with the public in a different light — taking into account the less tangible benefits that they are able to contribute to the relationship (such as co-operation, compliance or co-production), rather than thinking only in terms of a homogenised group of recipients of transactional services, the nature of which were devised by government.

It's a perspective that highlights the fact that we serve multiple 'publics', and it can help to shape our current understanding of the respective and sometimes competing claims of these different types of citizens, and how they are interconnected. It prompts us to explore ways in which we can enhance the outcomes for one group without diminishing them for another.

The current focus should be more about the effectiveness of service delivery. For the human services portfolio, it has meant seeing ourselves a bit like the online store Amazon — a large, national delivery system within which niche products not only exist, but piggyback on the system, enabling it to flourish. That means that we need to do our core transactional government business well, and add on extra services and information in ways that are packaged to suit people's particular needs.

The role of government

The changing nature of the interaction between governments and citizens the world over has given rise to considerable theoretical debate about the role of the state in modern society. Questions in this debate include:

---

4   Terry Moran, 'The Quiet Revolution — Observations on public policy', IPAA Seminar (May 2005).

- How do we raise the bar for everybody, including those with complex needs, and the majority who just want to get on with their lives and have little to do with us?

- How do we practically have both deeper and wider relationships with people in order to design better services?

For some commentators, a combination of socio-economic and political factors, such as privatisation, globalisation and the demand for governments to respond to 'wicked or intransigent problems', together with the growth of networks, has resulted in a weakening of the power and influence of governments.

According to this school of thought, government has become just one of a multiplicity of actors, and this has undermined its ability to control the policy process. This is called the 'hollowing out of the state', denoting a shift away from the traditional, centralised focus of government to more of a society-centred perspective. There is even discussion of the emergence of 'governance without government'.

Others argue that this society-centred perspective is overstated or flawed. Stephen Bell and Andrew Hindmoor take the view that, although governments are now demonstrably more likely to forge relationships with a larger range of non-state actors, they nevertheless remain the central players in governance arrangements.[5] Indeed, they argue that governments have been strengthened through the relationships that they have developed.

Whatever position one takes, a confrontational question flowing from this debate is whether genuine citizen or people-centred approaches can happen 'in the system'. In other words, can the public sector be the agent to develop the sort of community capacity required for real change, or does it need to step aside sometimes?

Evolution of service delivery reform in Australia

At this point, it is useful to remind ourselves that the push for services that are more responsive to the needs of citizens is not a new development. 'Citizen-centred' may have become a buzz word in the past decade, but the concept it embodies has a long history.

When a 1976 government inquiry (the Coombs Royal Commission into Australian Government Administration) reported on the need for public sector reform, a major concern was that the public service was less responsive to

---

5   Stephen Bell and Andrew Hindmoor, *Rethinking Governance: The centrality of the state in modern society*, Cambridge University Press, 2009.

changing community needs than it should have been. This led to a number of important changes in public administration, including more responsive service delivery. The past 30 years or so has seen a continuing trend away from a rigid, entitlement-based service delivery model to more flexible, place-based and individually tailored approaches.

Indeed, the 'simple but powerful idea' behind the creation of Centrelink in 1997 was: '… to make it easier for citizens to do business with the government, as opposed to pursing a mode of operations convenient for those delivering the service'.[6] The question, though, is whether progress in this evolutionary process has been rapid enough in recent years. We have been calling for new approaches for quite some time now.

While I am extremely proud of what has been happening in the portfolio I left in mid-2011, I am not sure that the public service as a whole has proceeded into that new era as quickly as I might have liked. It is very easy for public servants to keep on doing things the way they always have, rather than to think and behave differently. I am constantly struck by the view that, rather than embrace change, people want to be resourced to deliver something different. Transformation requires not only structural change, but behavioural and cultural change. It's time to push on even more rapidly with implementing this new paradigm. The community is impatient for change and the Internet and almost daily new information technologies provide the potential for transforming our institutions very rapidly.[7]

International context

Our service delivery reforms are, of course, part of the ongoing evolution of public administration in general. Given we now operate in a global environment, it's logical that the reforms we are experiencing in the APS are echoed in other developed nations around the world, as well as in other Australian jurisdictions.

Last year, Canadian academic Kenneth Kernaghan undertook a comparative study of international innovations in service delivery.[8] He observed that the international exchange of good practices in service delivery has had a major impact on service improvement initiatives around the world. For example, New Zealand's Kiwis Count, a national survey of citizen satisfaction with public services, is adapted under license from Canada's Citizens First surveys.

---

6   Australian Government (Management Advisory Committee), *Connecting Across Boundaries — Making the whole of government agenda work*, Commonwealth of Australia, Canberra, November 2010.
7   They also intensify the pressure for government to perform at the 'speed of the Internet.'
8   Kenneth Kernighan, *International Innovations in Public Sector External Service Delivery*, Treasury Board of Canada, March 2010.

He also pointed to Malaysia's use of mobile devices for service delivery and the open government initiatives of the United Kingdom and the United States as developments that could easily transfer to Canada. In Australia we are also looking for inspiration in what is happening in other countries. Indeed, the new Local Connections to Work program, which was recently introduced through a DEEWR/DHS partnership,[9] is based on a model that began in New Zealand a few years ago.

Canada has merged many of its government shopfronts and integrated phone numbers and websites to provide customers with themed information based on life events, such as 'finding a job' and 'raising a family' initiatives. In Australia, we have considered similar approaches and are co-locating many of our frequently used offices so that people can access more services in one location.

Through this joining-up, we are also expanding access to services to those in rural and regional areas who might previously have had to travel hundreds of kilometres to their nearest Medicare office. We are also expanding some of our own successful innovations, like mobile offices that are deployed quickly in emergency situations.

Are we doing enough?

Government in Australia is making clear progress in moving towards citizen-centred services, but the challenge is that expectations of government are growing at an even faster rate. At the time I stepped down as CEO of Medicare Australia in July 2012, some 34 Medicare Australia and Centrelink offices were offering integrated services, and a single phone number and single website for the portfolio had been launched. By the end of 2014, the intention is for around 570 offices to be providing integrated services.

Initiatives to allow people to take action themselves are also being pursued. Increasing numbers of transactions can be completed on line; for example, electronic claiming of Medicare rebates has recently been introduced, and existing online customers can now use a single login for all the human service portfolio's services. Over time, many more self-service options will be introduced to ensure better, more consistent service through all access channels and, better still, we will do most of the work behind the scenes.

---

9   The partnership between the Department of Employment, Education and Workplace Relations and the Department of Human Services.

New forms of dialogue with service users, the community, providers and intermediaries will help to reality-test whether what is being done is what people want to see happening. This is the very different and necessary perspective the Department of Human Services is taking to deliver twenty-first century service.

What does citizen-centred service look like?

Discussion of big reform initiatives can be pitched at a lofty level, but, in the end, it all comes down to making things better for people. Hearing people's stories and thinking about what can be done to improve their lives in a practical sense helps us to take a reality check on the goal to be achieved.

Take the situation of a family learning that their child has a disability. Their immediate priorities are usually about getting help for their child. The parents may or may not know where to turn first, and this is where a linked-up approach will come into play. And, while the Australian Government won't deliver all of the programs that parents may require, they will have ideas about who does and, consequently, should be able to link the parents to the relevant sources of help at the local level, particularly as the child moves through school.

While the parents are focusing on the needs of their child, government can help to ensure that their personal needs are met too, such as through coordinated and streamlined access to income support or ancillary payments, Medicare rebates, referrals to respite services or other programs to increase their wellbeing. By thinking and acting to address the needs of the entire family, the government can help protect them from the financial and personal pressures that can so easily impact on their relationships and health. This sort of preventive and caring service is what true citizen-centred service is about.

This example shows what an 'outside in' approach can mean for people and how collaborative schemes involving government working together with people and service professionals and the 'not-for-profit' or 'third sector' can improve public service delivery in ways that rigid program structures fail to do. By integrating sources of information around life events or local services, and providing things like 'warm' transfers (inter-agency/program facilitations) to other services for those with multiple, complex problems, overall wellbeing is improved.

To support this approach, we are moving to embed co-design principles in our operations. In simple terms, co-design is a systematic approach to understanding our customers and working with them to design, shape and deliver better services. Co-design is about the transfer of power from provider to user. Transferring power involves a shift in obligations and responsibilities, something that has to be negotiated between the government and the person receiving the service. To manage that shift properly, we need to understand the people we assist; we need to see the world and their lives just as they see them.

It follows that, if service quality and effectiveness is to be improved in ways that focus on the citizen, then citizens also have obligations. This extends not only to complying with rules, but also to people changing their behaviour and accepting responsibility for the choices they make, including the bad ones.

This approach is reflected in Australian social inclusion policies in which one of the principles is a greater voice, combined with greater responsibility, which is further articulated when people feel that they have a responsibility, indeed an obligation, to take part and to make progress. We need to work with people to design a government system that will ensure citizens are motivated to take responsibility.

A shift away from the control culture within government is also required. Control is anathema to the creativity and innovation needed from public servants to get true transformation. We obviously need to work within the law and the parameters set by the government, but, at the same time, we also need the room to create real, local solutions.

Importantly, public servants will also have to accept that they don't always know best — or even, don't know at all and so should go out and actively seek ideas and input. Most importantly, they need to take time to make sure that they are asking the right questions. We can identify a virtuous circle here: co-design should enable us to offer better quality services, which in turn will generate better user experiences with those services. Through co-design techniques, we can then use these experiences to further improve quality, and repeat the cycle.

This virtuous circle will also help to influence policy, build trust in government and overcome some of the reluctance that certain individuals and groups in the community feel towards engaging with government agencies. If people can see that public servants are genuinely listening to their views and acting on what they say, they will be more inclined to take up opportunities for participation. They will also see that their ideas matter.

So, too, do policy advisers need to begin to engage actively with service delivery staff and the citizens using these services. This already happens, but not nearly often enough. Wouldn't it be grand to have the work of public service policy-makers and service deliverers or program managers fully integrated around the needs of citizens, rather than separated and disconnected, as is the case now? Getting feedback loops working well and being bold enough to invite service users into our design processes is fundamental to delivering citizen-centred services. The public service could and should be doing this much better.

Where to now?

To this end, I think it is important that a more analytical approach to service delivery is applied. Specifically, there needs to be:

- a greater focus on systems thinking and collaborative policy and program design; as part of this, we need to understand the overall impact of complexity and the fragmentation of services and related requirements on citizens
- use of communities of interest across public service agencies involved in service delivery, focusing on the intersections, how to better join up services, and sharing innovative approaches
- more sophisticated data to build a picture of what matters to people
- the active use of evaluation and prototyping to test different approaches to engagement and service coordination so that we have a more informed understanding of what works and what doesn't
- greater mobility between the public service and the community sector as a way of increasing mutual understanding.

If these steps are taken there will be scope to ensure change keeps happening. Co-design is interactive and, in time, it also becomes transformative as the sea of initiatives crystallise into major change.

Conclusion

In conclusion, while there are significant challenges ahead, there is a real appetite across the public service to tackle the challenge of shifting to more citizen-centric delivery. If we look at the results of the annual state of the service employee survey, it is clear that the majority of Australian Government employees are keen to be creative and innovative, and work collaboratively across boundaries to deliver quality outcomes for the people that they serve. They are sometimes frustrated by the systemic constraints they experience, but my sense is that they are champing at the bit to take justifiable risks and try out new approaches. I'm excited about the direction in which the public service is moving and very optimistic about its future.

8. Measuring Citizen Feedback and Gauging Citizen Satisfaction

Bette-Jo Hughes

On behalf of my colleagues in Canada, I am honoured to use my contribution to this volume as an opportunity to explore the work that we are doing in the field of citizen-centred service delivery. Australia and New Zealand are similar to Canada in many ways, and I think each country can learn from the other.

In reading *Staying Ahead of the Game*, the Australian Government's 2010 reform white paper for its federal public service, it strikes me that we could replace the country names and the document would be just as valid in Canada, as we are focused on similar challenges. Equally, I understand that the work undertaken by New Zealand's *Experience Research Programme* (or NZE) undertaken in the State Services Commission is having great success in providing evidence to inform improvements to service delivery in that country. The focus of both works is relevant in Canada.

As the Assistant Deputy Minister for Service in British Columbia (Service BC), I am a service delivery practitioner; I am responsible for operations that provide services directly to citizens, in person, by telephone and online. To give some perspective, British Colombia is the westernmost province in Canada, with a similarly sized population to Queensland and similar in geographic size to New South Wales. In my contribution to this collection of essays, I will be exploring the key factors that contribute to successful citizen-centred service delivery work in Canada in general and in British Colombia specifically.

In Canada, citizen-centred service is not a new concept. Consider that in 1996 the Canadian federal deputy minister's task force on service delivery models stated that:

> Citizen-centric service incorporates citizens' concerns at every stage of the service design and delivery process; that is, citizens' needs become the organising principle around which the public interest is determined and service delivery is planned.

Though this quote illustrates the fact that the concept of citizen-centric service delivery has been with us for a significant amount of time, the drivers that motivated this change in focus in 1996 are very similar to the conversations we are having today.

We are all reviewing our programs, we all have resource challenges, and we work with the expectations that if citizens are changing, then the public service needs to transform to address these issues. We have made a good start in the process. Specifically, we are focusing on the citizens' view of government services — looking from the outside in — and we are taking citizens' concerns and needs into account at every stage of design and delivery. The next phase, which is a key theme in this volume of essays, is how we truly engage people in the conversation — not just asking how they are doing, but involving them, from the beginning, in the design of policies and services.

Figure 1: How government service looks from the outside-in

Source: Author's research.

A significant body of research on this topic has become institutionalised in Canada. Service BC's own citizen consultation on this topic used a variety of modes of research including quantitative surveys, exit interviews, focus groups, and blogs with citizens and front-line service workers.

Our research shows that Canadian citizens expect as good or better service from the public sector than they do from the private sector. Citizens often need more than one government service — especially when dealing with life events such as birth, death, travel, unemployment and internal migration within Canada. Moreover, the research uncovered some disturbing findings about how Canadian citizens interact with and access their public services. Namely:

- 26 per cent of those interviewed did not know where to start to find the service that they needed (principal reason given: confusing web pages or services not well advertised).

- 23 per cent of those interviewed said it was difficult to access the people or information they needed (principal reason given: busy telephones, broken links, being told their query was 'not my department' by service staff).

- Citizens said they were often required to manage the 'white space' that exists between related services (e.g., service bundles/clusters).

Overall, public services in Canada received an average service quality score of 72 out of 100 from those interviewed.

The next challenge for the research is to think about the measurement of the entire service experience versus the transaction, especially as the delivery of services now occurs through public and private organisations such as community service organisations.

The research has also supported the growth and persistence of single-window service delivery, which is successful when we:

- focus on delivering the right service
- use the appropriate service channel depending on the type of service
- use the right resources depending on the complexity of the transaction.

What makes this work is a shared vision, and broad acceptance and support that there are many ways to get there.

We believe there are five factors that drive service satisfaction: timeliness, knowledge and competence, courtesy/going the extra mile, fairness, and outcome. When all five are performed well, we found public services score 87 out of 100; when one driver fails the score drops to 74 out of 100; when four fail, it becomes 37 out of 100. Timeliness is the most important driver across all services and the telephone channel remains the priority for improvement. Figure 2 shows the long-term trend for customer satisfaction in Canada for 26 services.

Figure 3 shows the structure of the system used in Canada. Service improvements for citizens occur when the process is operationalised in a repetitive cycle.

The Institute for Citizen-Centric Service (ICCS) is a collaborative venture that engages all three orders of government across Canada and which promotes and supports improved service delivery by listening to and acting on the voice of the citizen. Specifically, it:

- supports two national service delivery councils
- manages an inter-governmental research agenda
- gathers, preserves and disseminates knowledge and innovative practices
- provides universally applicable tools and learning content through the establishment of a common standard for measuring the efficacy of service delivery, as well as providing service certification and learning
- builds capacity.

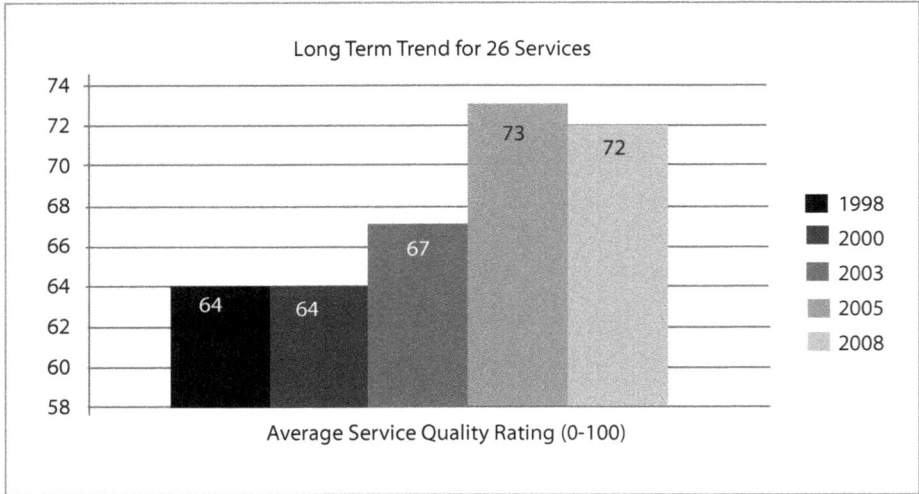

Figure 2: Federal, provincial, municipal service satisfaction performance trends

Source: Service BC, Government of British Columbia 2011.

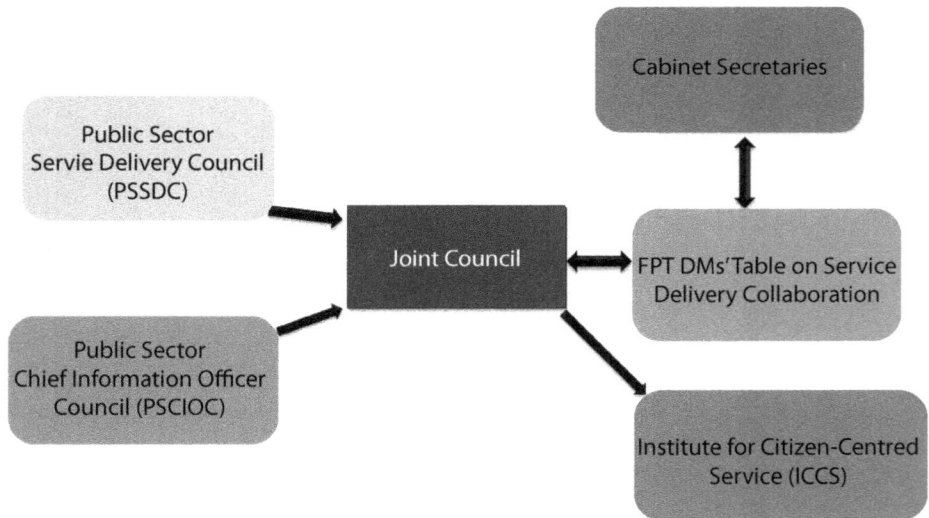

Figure 3: Service delivery community in Canada

Source: Author's research.

Specifically in British Columbia, our strategic decision-making is guided by our Gov 2.0 strategy, which was released in late 2010. Gov 2.0 outlines the focus on:

- empowering citizens to create value from government data
- saving citizens time in their interactions with government
- encouraging collaboration to deliver better quality services to citizens
- saving citizens time in their interactions with government
- encouraging collaboration to deliver better quality services to citizens.

British Columbia recently released our open government platform, *OpenData*. Learning from Australia's and New Zealand's open data websites, we hope *OpenData* will empower users to make better decisions that help people save time and money, help solve problems that matter in communities and encourage citizens and the private sector to innovate. After all, if we want citizens to engage with us in a dialogue about improving government policy and service delivery, we need to provide them with access to the same information that we have.

OpenData is the first provincial open data site in Canada and offers the largest number of data sets available on any government site in the country — nearly 2500 sets of data and growing, ranging from demographic information to education outcomes, fish habitat, and birth and death rates. The data is free, searchable and available for anyone to use. There is direction from our premier to ministries to continue to add more data and to think about the release of the data when they are building systems and reports. If we improve timeliness and access to services we will increase the trust of citizens in government.

OpenData is also the result of several citizen consultations. During these sessions, citizens expressed a wish that government would:

- provide timely access to services and information
- make services findable and user-friendly
- put the focus on services and the ability to get help from a government representative if needed.

We were also advised by the public to redesign our website, acting on the following suggestions to:

- move from a communications site to a service site
- emphasise the photo banner, which shows scenery from the citizen's local area, to inspire pride in the province

- move toward more life-event bundling (linking registries such as births, marriages, deaths and passport applications) and expansion of online services, and

- create a premier's page via which citizens can connect with their provincial government.

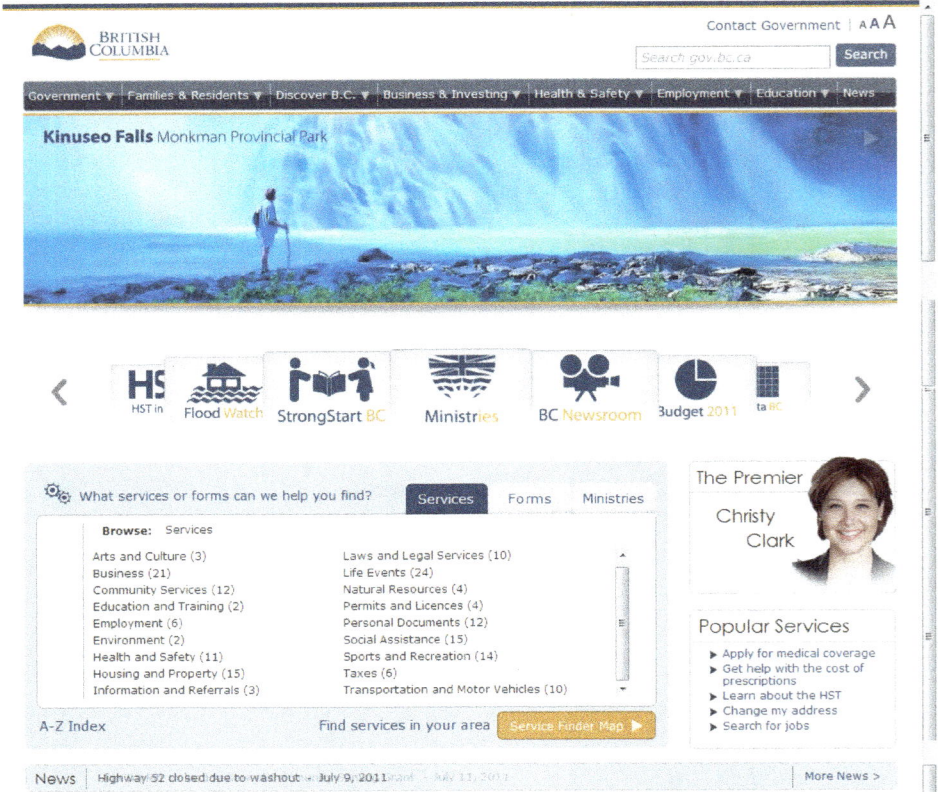

Figure 4: Official website for the province of British Colombia

Source: http://www2.gov.bc.ca/

We also encouraged collaboration with citizens for ideas to modernise the province's *Water Act*, a piece of legislation that is over 100 years old. The response was significant: nearly 27,000 visits to a purpose-built website and blog, as well as 500 people attending 12 face-to-face sessions across the province. Additionally, we received nearly 2000 submissions via blog, fax, email and mail over two phases of dialogue: one that sought input on what the *Water Act* could be, and one that put forward proposals for change to the existing legislation. The process is not yet complete; and a revised Act, with the focus on water sustainability, has yet to be legislated.

To paraphrase the eighteenth century Scottish philosopher David Hume, the magic happens when you connect policy development to people's passion, and that close contact creates empathy between government and the public through shared experience and understanding.

To conclude, I will outline some of the systemic lessons we have learned at Service BC during the process of improving service delivery in British Colombia. Namely, that:

- visionary leadership is essential
- paying heed to citizens' expectations and experience is fundamental
- research must be action-based
- ongoing measurement is critical to facilitating adjustments and sustaining engagement
- success rests on developing, nurturing and sustaining a spirit of community, partnership and collaboration
- creating a central platform for horizontal collaboration such as the ICCS is extremely important
- we need to be brave, try a new business process, utilise new technology, experiment with new business models and learn to take risks.

And, finally, here are some words of advice for fellow public policy practitioners:

- clear all content for approval expeditiously and build trust between communications personnel and program personnel
- being agile is critical, but it takes a lot of work on process to limber up
- invest in specialised software for text analysis to automate the process of sifting, sorting and categorising comments
- engagement can be a powerful tool that is applicable in many other circumstances.

I hope you heed these lessons and advice in devising your own modes of engagement.

9. Information Technology and New Media as Tools of Engagement

Martin Stewart-Weeks

What I intend to do in this chapter is briefly outline how we are starting to reshape and recast our conversations with citizens by using new technologies, and how this process is not only getting richer by the moment, but is often being driven not from within but from outside of the government.

First though, allow me to provide some background context. The head of the Department of Prime Minister and Cabinet Terry Moran said recently that, 'our processes should allow the community to provide input throughout the policy and service delivery process. Information technology can play a crucial role in facilitating communication between citizens and the government'. But I don't think we can understand the significance of what's going on in the conversation about new technology and what it's doing to the citizen–government relationship until we have a conversation about why. Why is this significant and what actually are these new techniques and these new platforms trying to achieve? What might they be driving or accelerating?

Distributed networking, the core architecture of the Internet, was essentially dreamt up in the 1960s when the big question in America was of maintaining the national communication system when Russia attacked (because, of course, we knew they certainly would). A distributing network was devised because, even if one of the communication nodes was brought down, the distributing network could still keep itself alive.

These are not suitable analogies, I think, for the world of government. Generally speaking, we have oscillated between these two systems — centralised and distributed. And generally speaking, we are learning how to operate in a distributing network — a process explored by Don Kettl (Chapter 3). And, while the early days of networking were all about control, our focus has now shifted to one of building resilience.

That is, essentially, what I would describe as the art and practice of connectedness: the notion that assets, culture and capability factors are having a fundamental impact on how we pull the two big levers that we've got available to us — innovation and productivity — to do better things and to do things better. Resilience, in my opinion, is about bouncing back from risk and from the mad, chaotic world we live in, all the while bouncing forward. How do we start to build societies that are more resilient in a proactive sense?

This sense of connectedness is very important. Nor is it the same as connectivity. Connectedness is about a culture of openness, sharing and co-creating; it's the art and practice of connectedness on which we need to focus.

My third observation is based on the work of business strategy consultant John Hagel who, with his team, have done some of the best thinking and writing about the information revolution. He talks about the increasing power of 'pull' in an environment that was once dominated by 'push' (the world of big governments and big corporations). At Cisco, we design and manufacture products, and then we get marketing people to go out and make you want the products. This is a scenario dominated by 'push'. Hagel argues that this once-dominant approach is gradually ceding to a world of 'pull', where people can use and get information, resources, insights, assets when and how they need them to suit their own needs.

Essentially, Hagel believes we are in a complete transformational refit process, including the underlying infrastructure (e.g., the National Broadband Network), the associated knowledge flows that they enable, and the traditional institutions of governments and markets. Of course, transforming the traditional institutions — their longstanding beliefs and mindsets is the hardest part of the refits process and I think we can learn some valuable lessons as to how to best do this in Kettl's chapter.

We are having richer and more meaningful conversations with citizens who are increasingly learning to live in the world of pull and are increasingly frustrated by the world of push. Much of this frustration with government is at least partially a function of the slow speed with which government is coming to understand that shift and acting accordingly. If you keep pushing at people who want to pull on their own terms, you're going to make them dissatisfied and unhappy.

Consider the recent work of Canadian Jocelyne Bourgon, a former senior public servant, in collaboration with the Australia and New Zealand School of Government (ANZSOG) and the Australian Public Service Commission. Called 'the New Synthesis', Bourgon is essentially trying to reinvent the business model for public administration in the twenty-first century. Her view is that public administration is no longer simply about compliance and performance. It is being transfomed into an area in which public servants and governments work to build resilience and anticipate emergent issues.

Another point is that we are living in a world where we are learning the power of the 'edge' (being 'out there' ahead of the pack). A few years ago a report written for the US Department of Defence asked: how do we turn the US defence machine into an 'edge organisation' and not a central organisation?[1] This is an interesting and somewhat ambitious aim. Edge organisations have a fundamentally different power topology from traditional organisations, as is clear from the contributions to this volume.

It is also a thread in many of the following examples. Consider firstly, that in late 2011 the ACT Government held its first Twitter cabinet meeting. It was an interesting experiment that resulted in close to 700 tweets being made over one hour, and 170,000 followers of the related hashtag in the same amount of time — that's almost half the population of the ACT!

The 'conversations' that emerged from this experiment were impressive. Topics they covered included transport, planning, human rights and gay marriage. Some questions were answered on the spot and some ministers provided impressive answers within the 140-character parameters of Twitter, and they often included a link. Other ministers responded along the lines of: 'Thanks for the question. We'll get back to you.' Such potentially unhelpful responses made the success of the experiment ambiguous. My favourite tweet, appearing at the end of the session, ran: 'What just happened?' I thought: 'Yep, that's pretty much the right question.'

Another example of an Australian institution making brilliant use of social media came during the 2011 Queensland floods, when the state's police force embraced Facebook as a medium for spreading emergency messages. It was an innovation on the run: major flooding and intense cyclones meant that there was no time for the police force to seek the relevant permissions through their regular channels. Faced with these challenges, the risk of using Facebook as a way of keeping people informed about developments — and to harness their views — was successful.

There have been other examples of innovative use of social media around the world. Ushahidi is a web-based platform that was initially developed to alert people to the outbreak of political violence in the aftermath of Kenya's disputed 2007 presidential election. Using open source technology on a simple website, it allowed citizens to provide geographical information about where violence was occurring. The platform has since been picked up in cities throughout the world for other purposes. In Atlanta, for example, it is used for mapping crime.

The North Atlantic Treaty Organisation (NATO) has also pioneered the use of social media. Last year, the organisation held a 'policy jam' that involved 4000 participants, 10,000 log-ins, 124 countries, five days, 10 streams, 26 online hosts and 75 facilitators. This last figure is a reminder that none of this spontaneous

---

1 M.S. Vassiliou, 'The Evolution Towards Decentralization C2', Institute for Defense Analyses, Washington, January 2010.

combustion happens without a complex choreography and preparation. That said, I suspect NATO has never had such a casual conversation about policy. Participants in the jam produced many ideas and suggestions and made particular recommendations, although it is not yet known how NATO has developed them.

In the United States, Cisco are working in a number of cities on the use of video technologies that can be uploaded to shared websites in a bid to reduce crime and violence amongst young people. It's about storytelling and capturing those stories on videos and uploading them onto a website where they can be shared and where they can spark conversation. Often, when we talk about greater engagement between citizens and government, we talk about the notion of citizens giving us feedback about our services. What I am talking about is different and it involves making the citizens the service and asking what we can do to enable that.

A point to make here, though, is that citizen engagement through technology is more about policy-makers waiting to hear from citizens. But, it is often more valuable for policy-making agencies to transfer information, which the public can then use, in sometimes unpredictable ways. It is doubtful that this is happening at the moment. Are the current efforts at citizen engagement creating services that people want, and delivering more effectively than any other model?

There are many companies now using complex online consultation mechanisms as a way of opening up the channels of dialogue between policy-making institutions and citizens. But it is not without risks. The Melbourne-based community forum Bang the Table gained notoriety in Victoria for releasing some sensitive information too early in 2010. This experience highlighted the potential risks when you start making the systems more porous, but nonetheless, it has been successful in most instances.

The United Kingdom, under the Conservative–Liberal Democrat coalition elected in 2010, is also busy opening up its channels for citizen engagement. In a bid to seek citizen input, the UK national archives are putting much of the material that they hold into the public sphere. In Australia, BetaWorks is a website that gives Australian Bureau of Statistics designers a place to showcase what they're working on, in order to gain feedback from the public and make sure that it meets the needs of the public. In many cases, I think, the jury is still out as to how effective such approaches are, but again, improving the dialogue between policy-makers and citizens requires experimentation with new methods.

In the United States, Facebook users now have access to 'a citizen request tracker'. An updated version of the 'rat-catching model' that Kettl references in an earlier chapter, it allows users to report city issues (potholes, code violations, animal matters etc) and then allow them to track their requests and see whether action was taken. The geographic location of each report or sighting is shown publically, allowing other users to respond.

A surprising pioneer in new citizen engagement methods has been the US Patent and Trademark Office (USPTO). Recognising that it has a shortage of expertise in key areas within the organisation, the USPTO has started to use social networking technologies to attract a wider audience of experts who can help them assess patent applications. As somebody once remarked, the trouble with our organisation is that most of the bright people we really need don't work for us, so the question is how do you find them, how do you harness them and how do you connect to them?

To do this, it is important to redefine the notion of expertise. In the commercial world, as well as in government and in the worlds of research and development, large corporations are beginning to realise that the kind of expertise they want tests the parameters under which they operate. This is an important point because for governments, there are lessons to be learned about where and how to listen to people who don't fit within those particular parameters, but who have genuine expertise to offer.

This is a challenge for governments because asking people to adhere to proscriptive guidelines can't possibly work anymore. By using social media, or other new forms of technology, citizens will find 110 different ways to make sure that governments, or somebody, does listen — in ways which can seem counterintuitive and even dysfunctional.

My penultimate example comes from the Australian Centre for Social Innovation's annual 'challenge'. A recent winner was a website aiming to increase community interest about the issue of binge drinking amongst younger people. Called 'Hello Sunday Morning', the website relies on people to voluntarily make claims and commitments about the way they're going to manage and improve their drinking habits. They are also encouraged to share their drinking problems with other members of the online community. Hello Sunday Morning is a way of engaging citizens on the basis that they are the service, as opposed to somebody providing them with a service. Technology can make that both appealing and convenient. This approach is also growing rapidly.

Additionally, if you visit the Australian Government Information Management Office website you will find several examples of people who are beginning to use social technology and technology more broadly in different and experimental ways. All agencies — tax agencies, human service agencies, and others — are trying to reshape the conversation between citizens and government. I mention this as a way of highlighting that there are lots of places now that are beginning to aggregate this information.

I will finish by outlining what I think may come from all of this. My observation is that the big human interaction sectors of the economy, such as the worlds of banking, airlines, retail and other big commercial arenas, are having to learn the important lesson that, although our social networks are not omniscient, they generally know more about things than we do. The tables have turned.

My experience is that, generally speaking, the government and the public sector work from almost exactly the opposite presupposition — that *they* know more than the network does, and only occasionally will they let the network in (by running a survey, for example). This is shortsighted and unwise. We are talking about a massive new invitation to engage in a myriad of different ways, we must embrace this offer.

We are talking about a world in which power, control and authority are being devolved and dispersed. Accepting and adapting to this is a challenge for those organisations that are accustomed to having all of those things. This is not, however, an either/or world, nor is it necessarily a case of 'in with the new, out with the old'. Just because everyone's on Facebook and Twitter and just because the five biggest airlines in the United States now have two-and-a-half million Facebook 'fans', does not mean we should totally ignore our old approaches. Social networking sites have provided US airlines with the biggest customer sample those companies have ever had, yet this doesn't mean the predictable institutional mechanisms involved in running an airline suddenly just disappear.

The problem is that the world that is being unleashed by some of the technology that I have sketched is very different to the one we have grown accustomed to over the past 20 or 30 years. What we must realise, however, is that the Internet and its attendant social networking technologies provide coherence, scale and accountability, but in different forms to before. It is now incumbent upon the public service to understand and adapt to these new forms.

References

Bourgon, J. 2011. *A New Synthesis of Public Administration: Serving in the 21st century*. Kingston, Ontario: McGill-Queen's University Press.

Hagel, J., Brown, J.S. and Davidson, L., 2010, *The Power of Pull: How small moves, smartly made, can set big things in motion*. Basic Books.

Part III. Case Studies: Land management and Indigenous empowerment

10. From Little Things, Big Things Grow: The rise of Landcare and citizen-orientated land management in Victoria

Jenny Pequignot

The singer Paul Kelly's iconic song 'From little things, big things grow' is one of my favourite songs and, I believe, the perfect soundtrack for Landcare — a once little organisation of negligible significance that has grown to be a big one with wide-ranging influence. Landcare, a partnership between government (where I work) and landholders with its origins in Victoria, is the focus of this chapter. The essay is thus about both regional and environmental issues and, in particular, the results of a recent information-gathering exercise.

What is Landcare and how did it come about? Landcare is a collective of community-based and volunteer natural resource management groups, originally comprising a coalition of farmers in north-western Victoria working collectively on land degradation. From these beginnings, Landcare has expanded to become a 'movement', with an estimated 60,000 members in Victoria alone and another 40,000 volunteers in that state. Across Victoria, these individuals have divided themselves into over 1000 Landcare groups, further divided into 62 statewide networks.

Landcare is an example of a grassroots, community-led movement that has replicated itself across Victoria, across Australia and internationally. Moreover, the term Landcare no longer exclusively applies to groups that call themselves Landcare, but various other citizen-led conservation organisations such as 'friends of' groups and Coastcare.

The partnership with government that spawned Landcare was formalised 25 years ago by an exchange of letters between Joan Kirner, the then environment minister in the Victorian Labor government under John Cain, and Heather Mitchell, the then president of the Victorian Farmers Federation (VFF).

A major strength of Landcare is the breadth of local agricultural and environmental knowledge and expertise held by its members. Landcare groups are made up of people that live and work in the same community, and its members are generally involved for significant periods, providing a consistent and stable base with established networks in the community. This attribute is fundamental to developing locally relevant solutions to environmental problems, and also arguably makes Landcare a non-threatening way for landholders to get involved in making environmental improvements. After all, in the forum of Landcare, landholders work with peers, who they generally trust, whereas they may not have the same reaction to government involvement in the same issues.

Being an organisation with a local focus, regional differences exist from one Landcare group to another. These regional difference are evidence of the diversity of stakeholders with whom government needs to interact on issues that are relevant to Landcare. In Victoria, for example, Landcare groups in the north-west of the state are typically small-scale and restricted to few networks. In the south of the state, by contrast, Landcare has many networks, and is also a strong lobby group. Networks are important because they reduce the administrative burden on local groups.

The impact of Landcare

What are the outcomes of this community-led approach to land management? Firstly, Landcare plays a significant role in natural resource management because it mobilises latent local knowledge and capacity to enact both community and landscape scale improvements. Moreover, these environmental improvements are on both public and private land.

Another significant outcome is that social networks that are established through Landcare contribute to the health and wellbeing of communities, so Landcare connects people through a common issue or goal. Landcare groups and networks also work with other local people and organisations to help them with information skills, labour and financial support. Examples include partnerships with schools, community groups, businesses, local government, public land managers and state government agencies. At a private level, Landcare succeeds in addressing long-term land management issues for property holders in Victoria and beyond. Such examples include tackling salinity and fencing off stands of remnant native vegetation.

As far as the current context for Landcare is concerned, there is evidence of an ongoing decline in the state of our environment, which means that the organisation is busier than ever before. There are increasing pressures on the environment through climate change, flood, fire and drought. There are also increasing expectations about productivity and, therefore, more pressure on the capacity of land and increasing demand for clean water. As a consequence, Landcare's local and community volunteer sector is under pressure, with such people often filling a gap in small towns where some services, that are usually provided by other actors (such as local authorities, landholders or community bodies), have been lost.

Despite these increasing pressures, Landcare receives limited financial support from government and is also suffering from the consequences of rural migration to cities, which results in a loss of local knowledge and ties to the local community. And, while the so-called 'sea change' or 'tree change' is bringing new people into rural communities, they often have limited local knowledge and skills. We also see absentee landholders, and the consolidation of farm enterprises has sometimes meant that we have land managers, who are less connected with local communities.

Government involvement in Landcare

The current role of government in the running of Landcare is to essentially invest in the delivery of environmental outcomes for the public's benefit so, although we work with private landholders, what we are most interested in is the public benefit for the environment, which is achieved through the work performed by Landcare groups and networks.

Government also provides annual program funding, particularly for work on the ground, but it also helps Landcare groups and networks provide, capture, promote and share information through a portal, website and quarterly magazine.

In some respects, government is the junior partner in its arrangement with Landcare. Landcare's rationale for existence is not to assume the service delivery responsibilities of government. There are, however, mutual benefits for both parties, with local communities receiving funding and support, and government achieving positive outcomes for the environment and good value for investments — sometimes a fourfold return. Some Landcare groups provide additional support to government through emergency response work in the areas of flood and fire recovery. Moreover, Landcare has been used to liaise between local communities and social networks; for example, on issues such as mental health awareness in drought affected communities.

To achieve optimum outcomes, consultation is conducted between government and Landcare groups, networks and peak bodies to establish the issues to be addressed, and what they desire from government — a process in which I participated earlier this year. The information-gathering exercise involved 10 regional workshops, phone calls and an online survey.

Findings of the information-gathering exercise

An interesting aspect of this information-gathering exercise is that it was possible to identify some clear market segments: the peak bodies were interested in a single united voice to government, the networks were more interested in government recognising their capacity and using them to do pilot work, whereas the groups and the volunteers were more interested in receiving more money for on the ground, practical work.

We learned that all tiers of Landcare wanted consistent and longer-term funding for coordinators and facilitators. They wanted support for groups to maintain basic operations, such as insurance cover. Interestingly, they also wanted administrative requirements for project funding to be commensurate with their capacity; in other words that the current reporting requirements are onerous and difficult to comply with. They also wanted recognition that they play an important role in natural resource management and they made it clear to us that they want to be in partnership with government.

Another finding of the information-gathering exercise was a desire to demonstrate the achievements of Landcare among its members. Landcare groups wanted government to help connect groups and networks to share ideas and to learn from each other, and they were keen to strengthen partnerships with other areas of government. They also perceived themselves as providing support and a service not only to the Department of Environment and Primary Industries, but also to health and community services and local government.

An interesting finding from the exercise was that policy directions from government were sometimes seen by Landcare as having a negative impact on the success of its groups and networks. Those consulted were critical of the assets-based approach, according to which it is believed there is not enough money to effectively protect all environmental assets, so the policy involves identifying key environmental assets, then investing in their protection and improvement. From government's perspective this was seen as an improvement on the previous 'Vegemite spread' approach, which neither prevented wide-scale land degradation nor protected high-value assets. It was apparent from the response of Landcare members, however, that an unintended consequence of the assets-based policy is that Landcare groups working in areas not deemed to have high value assets have missed out on funding to address local priorities.

The findings of the information-gathering exercise highlight the tension between local concerns and state priorities, and more effort should be made by government to better understand what those local priorities are. This does not mean that government should not continue to invest in the key priority assets for the state, but there is an opportunity to work with Landcare groups and networks to better communicate why certain areas are key priority assets and how their local work connects to them. In some respects, such tension might be explained by the way a policy has been communicated — it may be a perception rather than a reality.

Landcare was also critical of market-based instruments. These were seen as undermining the fabric of volunteer activity where local landholders were paid to undertake natural resource management activities that formerly would have been carried out by volunteers working together. Consequently, government needs to establish if market-based instruments are building the capacity of local groups or hampering them.

And finally, Landcare stressed a desire to maintain its independence — something the membership saw as critically important to allow groups and networks to help themselves.

Issues to address

So, how might government respond to some of those issues? Firstly, funding for coordinators is an election commitment and is consequently something that will clearly answer a need within the Landcare community. Government will give consideration to the way in which it can meet the need for longer-term funding arrangements, particularly for larger projects. With regard to governance and reporting arrangements, this is an area of design in which capacity constraints must be recognised while, at the same time, retaining accountability. There is clearly, however, a need to reconsider the policy settings to ensure that they are responsive to local needs. Government should be addressing high-value assets and local priorities. The information that is coming through is that there is a real desire to have a partnership approach to regional planning that recognises the impacts of market-based instruments.

As much as Landcare is an example of a successful, citizen-orientated approach to land management, government input is critical to provide groups and networks with technical and scientific information — something they are not always able to develop for themselves. Government is also in a better position to assist with the sharing of information across groups and networks, and it needs to do this by accessing better information from regional communities and responding to it in a way that maintains volunteer capacity.

Conclusion

In conclusion, the findings of the Landcare community consultation confirm that, while the public sector has done much right, there is plenty of work to be done to improve the partnership with Landcare. The information-gathering exercise provided us with good information about what we need to do better, namely the need to recognise that groups and networks exist in their own right and have their own local priorities and purposes. Government must understand that there are regional differences between Landcare's volunteer groups, networks and peak bodies, and that each of these have their own, often differing priorities. Better pathways need to established for local information to be shared between regional and state planning networks. And, perhaps most importantly, government needs to recognise local community priorities by adjusting policy settings and streamlining government requirements.

It is important to recognise that the Victorian Department of Sustainability and Environment and Landcare share the common goal of improved land management practices. Working to maximise and nurture the mutual trust and respect that exists between the two organisations should be a priority. From the department's perspective, the community consultation and information-gathering exercise was valuable and insightful and, where Landcare is concerned, it needs to be repeated on a regular basis so as to ensure that policy design and implementation, and the investment of services remains relevant and appropriate.

11. Volunteers as Agents of Co-production: The example of NSW State Reserves

Peter Houghton

I have worked in the field of land and natural resource management for over 40 years and currently look after the State Reserves in New South Wales. I am currently co-producing service outcomes with local communities through the preparation of plans for the management of these public recreation reserves. My background is as a practitioner; and I have a wealth of experience working collaboratively with other public officers and co-producing services with members of the public. In my contribution to this volume I will outline the role of Crown lands in NSW and given examples of effective mobilisation of volunteers and how the general public can co-produce the delivery of service outcomes.

In New South Wales, Crown lands are all the land that is owned by the state government. It is administered under the *Crown Lands Act* and is managed by the Crown Lands Division, a part of the Department of Primary Industries (DPI).

In its 2010 annual report, the division outlined its aim as managing Crown lands to deliver better outcomes for the people of New South Wales — including the use of such land for public enjoyment. This last part of the aim — the focus on public enjoyment — is what I found most interesting, because this obviously greatly assists the ability to co-produce service outcomes and mobilise volunteers.

The division manages approximately 43.7 million hectares of land — almost half of the state. This land comprises 35,000 reserves; 17 state parks; 270 caravan parks and camping grounds; 6500 travelling stock reserves; eight major recreational tracks and trails; seven national surfing reserves; most beaches, estuaries and waterways; showgrounds; country and community halls; heritage assets including lighthouses; convict-built ports; public buildings; and historical mine sites. It is a broad portfolio, and obviously a significant interface with the public of New South Wales.

A number of the 35,000 reserves are managed under trust. And, of particular relevance to the topic of this chapter, are those which have a community trust board, managed by reserve trust managers. There are approximately 700 such boards statewide, and they are given responsibility for the care, control and management of their reserve.

Further, the network of state parks are what I believe to be an example of successful co-production. These parks are scattered throughout the state, on the coast and inland, but particularly by major water resources inland. They offer a range of facilities for public enjoyment including accommodation (caravan and camping facilities, cabins and so on). Seven of those are currently managed by volunteer community trust boards. These are the state parks of Belmont Wetlands, Newcastle, Lake Keepit, Wyangala, Grabine, Copeton and Burrinjuck (on one of the major water supplies in inland New South Wales) and Killalea (on the state's South Coast).

Each of these trust boards, like all the other trust boards that are associated with the DPI, enjoy a level of autonomy that includes allowing them to enter into leases and licenses, setting entry fees and accommodation rates, employing people to work for them and determining the development of the land. So, although they do not conduct their business for private profit, they aim to maintain a level of income to operate their day-to-day activities. Importantly, they are not a branch of a government department but the government works in partnership with them to benefit the community.

To be a member of a trust board is an honorary, volunteer position. Each board has at least three and up to seven members, and they are responsible directly to the minister administering the *Crown Lands Act*. The tenure of board members is determined by their capacity to stay in their position. A member of the board of the Burrinjuck Waters State Park has served for over 50 years; another, on the board of the Copeton State Park, has served for over 40 years. Obviously these two volunteers are enjoying their stint in co-producing outcomes. And yet, volunteers are not entitled to any financial benefits; they can recoup out-of-pocket expenses incurred for carrying out their duties, but they are not entitled to any payment for loss of time incurred while performing board duties.

Most volunteers want to be positive and make good things happen and the volunteers who have served on the boards for a long time are truly the heart and soul of those assets. Without them, the parks would not exist because the government simply could not physically manage all of them. And yet, because of that small percentage of people who want to do the wrong thing, there has to be some monitoring from the outside. To this end there are 20 regional officers around the state, each with the responsibility of looking after the trusts.

The volunteer-run system arose primarily because of the lack of public knowledge about access to the state parks. There was a desire to improve facilities within these parks and, in fact, a key barrier to that was a lack of coordination between government and the individual trusts. A breakthrough came with the establishment of the State Parks Trust Advisory Board.

To improve coordination, a dialogue was developed to provide an internal support network to enable strategic planning for improved park management.

The accountability and reporting regimes of the advisory board are self-regulated, and this has resulted in improved coordination and implementation of policies such as a comprehensive marketing strategy, where there is now a unified brand. An annual reporting system allows the DPI to monitor the improvements or otherwise in each park.

The adjustments that have been made include a greater focus on the issues affecting state parks so that we could address the concerns of the trusts. The successful marketing strategy has increased visitation over the last few years by at least five per cent in each year. Therefore, there is improved delivery of product ensuring the consistency, equity and accountability of those services.

In respect to central government agencies, they were neither an enabler nor a drag on these initiatives. Going into the future, however, I believe it is important for the State Parks Trust Advisory Board to establish linkages with both central and other agencies for the provision or the co-production of resources.

Both the department and the advisory board must obviously work in conjunction with private landholders throughout New South Wales whose properties border Crown land. In fact, we often have a close working relationship with the neighbours, particularly in rural areas of the state, where there is extensive need for weed control and feral animal control. In a few cases we have even developed our fire management plans only after consulting the neighbour's plans first, so as to make sure of having a coordinated effort across the board. As our trust boards comprise of volunteers, it also helps that they are often neighbours in their private lives to the same people who border Crown Lands.

The second example I would like to mention is the caravan and camping grounds. These are an excellent case of the public successfully participating in policy development and co-producing outcomes. This has been facilitated by the introduction of the Caravan and Camping New South Wales website. Again, as with the state parks, the opportunity to develop the website arose as a result of recognition by the public, as well as by departmental officers, of the need to improve those facilities. The key barrier to achieving that was a lack of a comprehensive database to inventory the condition of facilities at caravan and camping grounds on Crown Lands across the state. To rectify this, the caravan park operators and the division formed a partnership in order to survey the responses of caravan park users to the idea of such a database. These two groups also presented their plans for the database at camping shows. After this, the database was developed.

After permission was granted by each park operator to advertise their facility online, the website was then launched at a caravan and camping show in Sydney. We then established a newsletter with in excess of 20,000 subscribers, which serves as a mechanism for self-fulfilling accountability and reporting. Users have been encouraged to give us feedback, and that which we have received so far has prompted us to make a number of improvements. The feedback also provides the government with a way of monitoring compliance with government regulation so both the government and public benefit from better facilities.

The website certainly provided a focus for that. With the onset of social media, there will also be future opportunities to explore new linkages with existing and future legislation through this medium.

So, to conclude, I have two key messages. The first is to never promise something you can't deliver. Nothing dissuades potential volunteers from joining up like unrealistic commitments. Secondly, for volunteers to be effective, the organisation with which they work needs to be able to provide an internal functional support network to facilitate the ongoing activities of those volunteers. Without that support network the project will undoubtedly fail.

12. Indigenous Empowerment in Land Management

Mark Chmielewski

I manage the Indigenous Landholders Service (ILS), a program within the Western Australian Department of Agriculture and Food. Though the department has been in existence for over 100 years, the ILS has only existed for 13 years. We work with Aboriginal landholders and the approach that we take is to primarily employ Indigenous Western Australians from the state's remote communities, its pastoral industry, its agricultural industry and from within the state government itself. The current team is solid and has essentially been together for five years — a great retention rate.

Origins of the ILS

The Indigenous Landholders Service started 13 years ago at Noonkanbah pastoral station in the Kimberley region of Western Australia. Around 350 people live on Noonkanbah, which raises cattle. In 1998 the station's herd suffered a severe tuberculosis outbreak, provoking a visit from the Western Australian Department of Agriculture's Tuberculosis Program. Unfortunately, such was the severity of the outbreak that one of our officers had to destroy 1200 head of cattle. The loss took away the Noonkanbah community's ability to create employment and training — its ability to pay bills and wean itself off welfare.

Facing this crisis, Noonkanbah community leaders asked the visiting officer, 'What are we going to do now? How are we going to pay our wages? How are we going to employ our people?' The officer thought about this, and promptly went beyond his scope. He was there to address the tuberculosis outbreak — not the needs of the community. And yet, the officer sat down with the community and together they developed a pastoral management plan. He recognised that there were some inherent weaknesses and governance shortcomings in the way Noonkanbah was being run. Consequently, there were a range of negative issues affecting the local residents. So, from this meeting between that particular officer and the community grew the Indigenous Landholders Service.

From those humble beginnings it has grown to become an incredible success. At that point Noonkanbah was a couple of hundred thousand dollars in debt. Today they are still receiving an extension service, but they are now putting close to $2 million back into the community. Importantly, Noonkanbah is employing people in remote Australia. There are young, primarily Indigenous, people coming up through the education system who want to go and work on that property that may have otherwise ended up on the welfare cycle. In that sense Noonkanbah is providing an opportunity for a bright future for young Indigenous people in the Kimberley, and an opportunity for those who have already fallen into welfare dependence to lift themselves out of it.

Beginning at Noonkanbah 10 years ago, the ILS now encompasses 77 properties. There are still more properties out there needing access to our services, but we simply cannot assist them because of a lack of government resources. And yet, we have still been able to enact what is nothing less than a revolution in service delivery.

Unfortunately Western Australia has a history of what I call 'unserviced' landholders. While repatriated soldier settlers returning to the state after World War I and World War II were given low interest rate loans and Department of Agriculture support to accompany their land allocation (business management, cropping, machinery and animal husbandry advice), no such support was given to the next wave of repatriation — to Aboriginal people in the 1970s, 1980s and 1990s, who were allocated pastoral stations and farms to go to. Consequently, 30 years after these first waves of Indigenous repatriation, the ILS is trying to redress some of the problems that have accumulated in the ensuing decades.

Approach of the ILS

The approach of the ILS is a holistic one: focusing on people and developing relationships between them. Everything else fits around this method. When we go to properties, we have a couple of major themes to help us succeed. One is an emphasis on the development of skills and knowledge within a community, so that they can make informed decisions regarding their own governance. This can be achieved through training.

Crucial to this is the desire for employment, and the opportunity to create employment. To do this we sit down with the community or corporation in question and work through what it is they want to achieve out of the property. There is no one answer to this question, but essentially it is about designing and implementing a communal goal for the landholders.

For this to be successful, a long-term approach must be undertaken — we are consistently trying to convince government to look beyond the election cycle; that a three-year turnaround on this issue is unrealistic. This is about generational change. The ILS is also beneficial to the Department of Agriculture because it increases property productivity.

We are held accountable for the public dollars that we spend in each ILS project and, as well as paying for independent evaluation and validation of our work, we also conduct internal assessments from within the Department of Agriculture. These come in the form of quarterly reviews, bi-annual reviews, annual reviews and two-year reviews. Though this process sounds very bureaucratic, we do not lose sight of the fact that we employ a grass roots approach that runs parallel to a strong evaluation and justification purpose.

We are an invitation-based organisation. As a consequence, when a corporation says to us, 'can you come and help us with our land, we are struggling', we sit down and we attempt to understand the people; we try to understand their story. We identify what skills they have, before starting to develop a property plan. Then we assist with governance because governance and business support are mutually beneficial. If you have one without the other a lopsided equation can eventuate, and this can hamper the betterment of the community in question.

Essentially though, the success of an ILS-serviced property depends on us being able to initiate developmental plans and structure training, identify the weaknesses and strengths, then assist the corporation to move above and beyond where it wants to go. We have our partners in this. Though the program started off as a collaboration between the WA Department of Agriculture and the communities, over time it has developed to the point where it has become a cross-government, holistic service and other government agencies are now climbing on board to assist in the implementation of their activities as well.

The Indigenous Land Corporation, an independent statutory authority of the Commonwealth government, is a funding partner of the ILS program. The communities themselves are obviously the major stakeholders, and then a whole range of agencies further down the tier are also involved in the work that we do. Because of the agencies and activities that are now involved, coordination is critical — there is nothing worse for a community than to see a stream of 4 x 4s come in and out over the course of a week, with each agency wanting to deliver their own outcomes. Because of this, through a process of evolution, the work of the ILS has become structured around a system of property management so we can assist the other agencies involved to deliver an effective service.

Impact and outcomes

The 77 properties we service provide land to 4000 people, and it is their lives that are most impacted by the management and use of the land on which live on. While these people may not all get a job thanks to the ILS, they have certainly been given training opportunities as a consequence of our involvement. Milijitty and Lamboo are two successful examples of pastoral properties that have benefited from their relationship with the ILS, and where the custodians now exhibit a real sense of pride in their station and community.

Economic outcomes are the most significant impact the ILS has on the properties it serves. I have highlighted Noonkanbah as a successful example earlier in this chapter, but there are many other, similar, case studies. Noonkanbah's neighbouring properties are an example. They are also Aboriginal communities and they also have many people associated with their land. These properties have been able to replicate what their next-door neighbour, Noonkanbah, has achieved: they are now starting to implement their own goals and their own objectives — processes we are helping to facilitate.

There are also regional implications of this scheme. Often, when an Indigenous-run property falls into debt, there are negative flow-on effects for the region as a whole. We have come to properties, for example, that haven't paid bills, and the local helicopter pilots or the livestock agents or the truckers have told us, 'we're not touching that property, we've been there, we've got a $7000 bill, they haven't paid it. Forget about it'. Such a situation is not good for anybody. But, what we have equally found is that, through the ILS facilitation process, once these properties start developing their business and generating some cash, they can repay that debt and repay some of that lost faith. Consequently, once the community has won the trust of mainstream service providers, the commercial world can come onboard as a mechanism for reconciliation.

There are truckers, for example, now actively engaged in transporting cattle from Aboriginal-owned properties. There are helicopter pilots now recognising and acknowledging that these properties have instituted strong corporate governance, and so they are once more servicing them. In this way, the regional roll out and fan-out effect is considerable.

A number of the properties that we worked with have achieved self-sufficiency in a short period of time, which is something that brings with it its own set of challenges. From not having any money in the bank, these properties now have to understand the varying responsibilities associated with having $10,000, $100,000 or even $1,000,000 in the bank. In addition to becoming financially literate, these properties have to also deal with the challenges of creating a business in an environment where basic literacy and numeracy is still a major issue, and to assist in implementing structures that protect the investment of their corporation in a trusting way, without it being unfairly exploited by outsiders.

As the properties have developed, 55 full-time and 83 part-time jobs have been created. While these figures may not sound world-beating, each one represents a person who has come off welfare and who is now involved in their own businesses, on their own land.

Take the case of Robin, a man from Halls Creek. Robin grew up in a humpy on the edge of town with no electricity or running water — a very different upbringing to most Australians. He used to walk a couple of kilometres to school — when he wanted to attend. There was no real incentive for him to go to school in Halls Creek. He started life much like his peers and by the time he had reached early adulthood, Robin was abusing alcohol and engaging in anti-social behavior.

Fortunately, at this stage, Robin's father sent him to agricultural college in Katherine and, while he didn't graduate before returning to Halls Creek, he gained enough knowledge in pastoral business for us to engage with him and convince him to apply his skills in his home community.

Robin doesn't drink anymore. He's since completed his diploma in agricultural science and become a leader in his community. He still lives in Halls Creek, from where he runs a pastoral station and is the chair of his corporation. He is an example of an Indigenous Australian who has taken a land asset that was depreciating in value and restructured it into something more positive (and lucrative). Now all his nephews are standing around looking at Robin saying, 'I want to be just like my uncle', they are lining up to go to school. These are little steps, but they prove we making progress.

And, while such outcomes are heartening, we must equally recognise that agriculture is not necessarily the professional pinnacle for all Indigenous Australians living in remote areas. Often it is a just a starting point. John, a former shearer from Albany in southern Western Australia, is a good example. Much like Robin, John dropped out of high school and got into the welfare cycle. But then he became involved with some of the properties we work with, where he realised he enjoyed — and was very good at — shearing. He was shearing about 150 sheep per day, which is impressive for a first-year shearer. In addition to this skill, John developed an impressive work ethic and, after starting as a trainee, he was soon accepted into a commercial shearing contracting team.

Having acquired that work ethnic through agricultural experience, John, who is only 23, has transferred it to Western Australia's mines, where he now drives heavy machinery. He is earning good money, and is leading a good life.

Like Robin, he has become a role model for young people in his community; a community he wants to give back to. Unlike Robin though, John's trajectory shows Indigenous kids from the bush that they don't necessarily have to end up in agriculture. His story is one of professional transformation, and the ILS can assist in that process.

Cultural outcomes

Cultural awareness is obviously important in what we do, and critical to the success of the ILS. Near the town of Meekatharra, in the middle of Western Australia, there used to be a pastoral station. The WA Department of Agriculture thought it was running smoothly until the day we decided to see for ourselves. Because Aboriginal people tend not to attend field days, they generally don't think to pick up the phone and call the department when they have a problem. So, unless we visit these properties for ourselves, a large group of people don't have access to the department's services. When we arrived at the property, the management said that they did in fact have problems. We conducted an inspection of the property and confirmed that these problems were so severe that they were putting the community at risk of losing their property altogether.

This community didn't want to run a property, but, rather, it wanted to maintain it for cultural reasons. They were from that country; they were born there; they had stories that were attached to that country. So they wanted to retain it in order to maintain their sites, continue their law and continue to teach their children about their culture. Once we understood this, representatives of the ILS met with custodians of the property to devise a model whereby management of the property was outsourced, but the community could still maintain it for cultural purposes. This was achieved through sub-leasing.

Under this arrangement the property's next-door neighbor subleases the land, improves the infrastructure and runs his cattle on it. The contract stipulates, however, that the landholders can have access to the country whenever they need to in order to maintain their cultural sites or educate their people. Equally, they can stay at the homestead during these occasions and have first priority of any employment and training outcomes attached to the pastoral use of the property. It is thus a win/win situation. It is understood that the men of that particular corporation had given up using the land for agriculture, but their women convinced them to find a way of maintaining it. As a result we have a situation where, in 15 years' time the land is still there for the grandchildren to take over the lease, should they ever wish to do so.

This example also highlights the benefits of taking the time to visit a community and ask them if they have any problems. Often, when departments use the word 'engagement', what they mean is engagement with a particular agenda set by the community. But, at the ILS, we have learned that when you sit down with a community, the issues are often so much broader than initially anticipated and require meaningful, two-way engagement. Not a lot of departments put the time, effort and energy into sitting down and understanding the needs of communities — something that can take a long time.

When it comes to Indigenous–government engagement, there remains a significant level of mistrust. Consequently, these meetings can often take hours before the talking actually starts. It's unrealistic to expect people to declare their issues in the first couple of meetings; instead we have to tease them out and use different methods to establish exactly what their issues are.

The challenge of gaining executive and institutional support

The ILS is not without its detractors. While the key trigger for the creation of the service was the development of a relationship between a government employee and a community, the scheme's development and sustained success has depended upon support at a higher level: within management, within the executive, from the department's head and from the WA minister for agriculture. As an innovative approach to Indigenous land management, this has not always been straightforward.

The, sometimes difficult, process has involved making such people and institutions aware of the innovation at work, and in so doing finding a champion to drive the process and keep a particular project going. For a long time, what we do flew under the radar in the corridors of power in Perth, but there was only so long before the success of the program became known, even to those who, for whatever reason, may not want to be convinced of its virtues.

And while the ILS has not been entirely endorsed yet — the WA Department of Agriculture is conservative — the program's success to date has been such that it continues to shift peoples' attitudes to this issue, meaning we continue to gain champions for our cause.

A national and international role model

From its simple beginnings at Noonkanbah station, the ILS has grown to become a model of success to be emulated across Australia and the world. Not only has the United Nations recognised the work that we do, we are two-time WA premier's award winners for excellence in public service and also previous winners of the prime minister's award for excellence in public service. Interested parties from African nations have visited Western Australia to observe our activities, and the South African Government, in particular, is trying to implement a similar model in that country.

I am not aware of another service in Australia that delivers such a holistic approach; that sits down and breaks the mould of accepting what can and cannot be done. When liaising with other agencies we often get told, 'we'd love to help, but what you're doing isn't part of our agenda.' The ILS is about breaking this mentality by being innovative, entrepreneurial and committed in order to find ways to solve problems that have long been deemed too difficult.

13. Improving Indigenous Access: Three practitioner perspectives on citizen engagement

Adrienne Gillam, Ian Mackie and Michael Hansen

Adrienne Gillam: In examining improvements in Indigenous access I will discuss the Remote Service Delivery National Partnership Agreement, an initiative on which I have been working over the past couple of years. I will share with you some of the findings and lessons learned from this project, as well as outlining its aims and function. First though, I will provide some background to the initiative.

In 2006, former Aboriginal and Torres Strait Islander Social Justice Commissioner, Tom Calma, threw out a challenge to Indigenous policy-makers and practitioners: if we were serious about improving Indigenous access and about citizen engagement with Indigenous people, we had to make the effort to talk to them about service delivery. One need only consider the substantial media coverage devoted to the recent consultation process concerning what will happen at the conclusion of the Northern Territory National Emergency Response to see that this issue looms large in the Australian consciousness.

Calma's words, though spoken in 2006, resonate just as strongly today as they did then. In 2009, spurred on by his challenge, the Remote Service Delivery National Partnership was founded upon the realisation that if the whole-of-government objective of closing between Indigenous and non-Indigenous Australia is to be achieved, business would have to be done differently.

In the two years since, new approaches to improving Indigenous service delivery and access have been tried, with varying degrees of success. It has become clear that, if we focus on a specific location — a place-based approach — rather than pursuing a nationwide solution, it is possible to talk seriously about coordination and to do it properly. As a result, in the Northern Territory, 15 remote service delivery sites operate, and there are two in South Australia. There is evidence that these sites are effective.

The partnership has, therefore, focused on place. However, it is not being implemented everywhere. While there have been some failures, the South Australian minister for Indigenous Affairs has said: 'I want to test this methodology and if it works, then I want to roll it out more widely'. The specific nature of this approach makes it at the same time expensive, intensive, innovative and tailored. It is co-produced, being a partnership between all levels of government, the state and territory jurisdictions, the Commonwealth, and the community sector — including business, the NGOs and not-for-profit organisations.

South Australia has benefited from being able to test this 'place-based' methodology with communities of less than 200 people. It is a bigger challenge in the larger communities of the Northern Territory. Regardless, it is clear that the methodology is already achieving results.

The key feature of the 'place-based' approach is that government comes to the community. In South Australia, the secretary of the Department of the Premier and Cabinet at the time of the program's founding, Chris Eccles, ensured that for the two trial sites in South Australia, CEOs of 30 major departments came out to those communities and consulted with them, gauging their feelings, identifying their priorities and, more importantly, agreeing on what would be the actions in local implementation plans. These community-based plans are unique partnerships in the sense that Indigenous people in communities have devised, co-designed and co-produced all of the actions in the plans. Such a partnership, whereby everyone affected is a signatory, is unprecedented in an Indigenous portfolio. And, in the case of the Northern Territory government, the plan even goes to cabinet for approval and endorsement.

An important element of this methodology is that, in the communities involved, there is a single government interface — and a single coordinator. Indigenous people in the communities prioritise the sensible and seamless delivery of services ahead of which political party is in government, or what tier of government is involved (Commonwealth, state, local or shire).

As a consequence, in all of these sites in both states, a government business manager, who belongs neither to the state nor Commonwealth, operates locally. We also have Indigenous engagement officers who are the cultural ambassadors for their communities. These officers provide the links that are fundamental to doing business in these communities.

The fact that the business managers have a combined role can, however, be an area of tension. Sometimes Australian government agencies try and use a government business manager in a way that is contrary to their intended purpose. For example, the government business manager may be asked to deliver a program or run consultations for a particular government purpose. This tension must be finely balanced and we have attempted to achieve this by assuming that no one individual has the necessary skills to undertake all of the requirements of the role. Local skills and cultural and language requirements of the position are addressed by the Indigenous engagement officers. They are a key part of the mix.

As often as possible, government officials go to the communities in combined groups from various jurisdictions; often our staff go out together with their Northern Territory equivalents as an active partnership. The board of management for the program is co-chaired and is also undertaken as a partnership. The government business manager is given the clear understanding that they belong neither to the state nor to the Commonwealth, but, rather, are responsible for the coordination of government services, whatever their branding.

How do we prepare our officers for their roles? Appointments are generally made of individuals from a multidisciplinary background, mostly with tertiary qualifications, if not with postgraduate qualifications. The current, best performing government business managers are those who were Canberra policy bureaucrats and who know the system, but have come to the conclusion that the only way to understand how Indigenous communities work is to immerse themselves in one for a year.

There has also been an evolution in the kind of government business managers that have been appointed. Following the 2007 Northern Territory National Emergency Response (widely known as 'The Intervention'), instituted by a Coalition government under John Howard, we tended to have a lot of police or army personnel — people who were good at maintaining law and order or re-establishing functional governance in a particular place. But now we are moving on from that to attract a skill set which is more community-orientated.

We train personnel by immersion and support them *in situ*; there is no other way and we do not need to apologise for it. You do have to live in Wadeye to understand Wadeye's clans, and the same goes for every other community. We can read reports and even theses on local communities, but they are not substitutes for being there and understanding how they work.

Some induction training is necessary. In the past, people going into the communities have said to us: 'it would have been great if we'd had that training upfront'. We are now giving them some upfront skills during their induction. But we don't invest too much in cross-cultural training, because we think it is only useful to someone who is going to have very limited interaction with a community. Everything is so culturally specific to where you are placed. People tend to forget just how diverse Aboriginal Australia is: the 15 sites we service are distinct; there is no one size that fits them all, meaning there is no substitute for time with a particular community.

We have also learnt that we need to use skilled and trusted practitioners who have come through our tertiary institutions or have learned by working with practitioners who have spent time living in communities. All our South Australian staff involved in the partnerships undertake a Pitjantjatjara language course to be able to communicate effectively. I speak and understand the Pitjantjatjara language, and I expect all my staff who go out and do community work in Pitjantjatjara country to have an equal measure of proficiency in the language.

In the Northern Territory we have no hope of doing that, because there are 104 languages. So, where it is achievable, we have set out to learn the local language. When it is not feasible to learn the local language, we use a professional interpreter service in the Northern Territory to engage with the community. A good example of this recently was when we were conducting consultations about the Northern Territory National Emergency Response. A common theme of those consulted was a hatred of the BasicsCard system, whereby cardholders have their income managed and can only spend money at government-approved stores and businesses. But when we, with the help of interpreters, sat down with six or seven groups simultaneously and asked them what specifically it was about the BasicsCard they did not like (and bearing in mind the negative coverage it had received in the media) we found their concerns were relatively small irritations — like not being able to tell how much credit was left on their card and other such easy-to-fix issues.

So, through this process of community consultation with skilled practitioners, we discovered that it was not the policy initiative per se to which the opposition was directed. In fact, we found that many people actually like the system of income management instituted during the Northern Territory intervention, because it quarantines their funds from being utilised by other people (or from being accessed by other people, or from being spent on things that they would not have chosen to spend it on). And they liked the idea that it could buy food and clothing — they just did not like a minor informational aspect of the card. We were able to pass this finding on to our Centrelink colleagues and try and devise a scheme whereby people could access their card's balance before they go shopping. And, it turns out, there are various means of doing that.

While all this engagement on the ground may sound daunting, communities are great educators. I am always struck at how patient and how pragmatic they are. And truly, if I personally saw the endless parade of bureaucrats that come to these communities, I think my patience would be more limited than theirs. But they are always prepared to educate, to inform and to include you. This is a huge part of the education process.

Today, our partnership engagements are backed up by strong governance supports. We recognise, through a wealth of previous research that, if we do not have strong governance underpinning the national partnership — as well as the community — we face an unassailable challenge.

We recognise that our partnerships — between government representatives and specific communities — are ones between equal partners from unequal places. So, how do we make sure both partners in the agreement are equal? Firstly, we make it clear that the communities involved are indeed equal partners. In devising actions and priorities for local implementation plans, the relevant community will have a say in aspects of the plan and, in some instances, it has a bigger say than the government agencies. What gets into local implementation plans is contested ground. As a result, every development is critiqued and the final product can take a long time to be finalised. In the Northern Territory alone there are close to 3000 actions still waiting to be dealt with that we could not put in a local implementation plan because no consensus could be reached on the issues that were being addressed.

The bigger tests will be if the community does not do their part; what then is the penalty? Or what will happen if the other partners want to change the agreement? And we have had these things happen, forcing us to go back and renegotiate. But, because we have managed to develop a trustful relationship during the engagement process, we can go back and be honest with the communities and say: 'Look, we said we were going to do those roads, but because of X, Y and Z, it's not going to be achievable in that timeframe. So we need to renegotiate it'. Or we say: 'What's negotiable? What can we work with and what can't we?'

In one example, the ink was barely dry on one of the South Australian local implementation plans when an agency wanted to withdraw something from it. It was such a long and negotiated process that I was astonished that anyone, at that point, would seek to withdraw it. But it is a measure of the agreement process we now have in place now that officials cannot just come along and say: 'We're taking out this thing now, sorry about that, and we'll tell you about it later'. That is why a specific accountability measure, called a 'local implementation plan tracker', is in place. It reports to the board of management of every state, territory and Commonwealth agency. It does not matter if it reports things are on or off track, on time, on budget — they are all reported in implementation tracker. And, from my experience, this is the first time that we have had such a system of checks in place, enabling us to go back to the community and say: 'Hang on, we've done our two things. We've built the childcare centre; we've put in the staff, now you've got to get the kids there every morning. That was your bit of the deal'. Moreover, we have a trusted, honest broker in town, who can have these tough conversations and tell the truth — and as one of my colleagues keeps saying: 'You've got to tell the truth till it hurts.'

One of the immediate benefits of the National Partnership Agreement is that we have been able to do considerable work on mapping overall services that are going into communities, not just baseline provisions. We now know what goes into each community and, by understanding that, we can start to see some of the synergies, capping or duplication. The problem of duplication, after all, is a common one. People in the communities are continually saying to us: 'Don't send out another youth program. Don't send us another financial management program. You governments need to get your act together'. This is an important message. These communities do not want seven or eight separate programs coming in simply because someone external to the community decided they would be beneficial to the community. They want wraparound services suitable to their needs.

Slowly but surely, we are learning from the communities themselves what works and what does not. Though this approach — learning from service user feedback — may work in small communities, it is more challenging when dealing with a greater number of sites. For this reason we have local, on the ground participatory research to scrutinise, measure and report back to government which services are working, rather than merely congratulating ourselves for improvements we perceive to have made in, for example, education or health. The community has a set of measures and can decide for itself whether improvements have indeed been made.

Not only is this community appraisal important to us as a source of feedback, it is important because it allows us to summarise the trends and problems and then canvas the community for possible solutions. For instance, while we might have data that says 'school attendance is stagnant,' it is not as valuable as insider input. Local research, from local people who are trained and who know how to collect data and do surveys — quantitative and qualitative — can say, 'Well, actually, no, we've got some measurable improvements here in these years at these grades, or in these cases there are improved attainments'. So we get better quality information. Most importantly, the community can then feel empowered when they say, 'Gee, we are doing well on these counts. Whatever we have been doing in relation to A, B and C initiative is paying off.'

Finally, fundamental to an improvement in the provision of Indigenous support services is our ability to listen. Often, during consultations, we are told, 'You come out and you talk to us, but you don't listen'. Many communities have made that point. They say 'You claim to listen but really what you are doing is coming back and telling us; your ears are getting smaller but your mouth is getting bigger'. In our Indigenous partnerships, we have to be mindful of that and continually strive to have bigger ears.

Ian Mackie: Although this volume of essays is dedicated to citizens' centricity in policy-making processes, and citizens being in control of their lives, my daily work involves dealing with a political discourse that is focused on issues of dependency, intervention, welfare reform and fines for truancy. It strikes me that the subject of this volume and my daily experiences are two competing worlds. Perhaps this disparity is due to a stark social reality: there is an ideal public sector provision for white people and another for black people. This proposition forms the basis of my contribution, with my reference point being Indigenous education.

Consider those factors that might be called the 'knowns' of Indigenous education in Australia. First, we know that over the past 15 years there has been an improvement in the provision of Indigenous education. There is, however, still a significant gap in the learning achievements between Indigenous and non-Indigenous Australians — a gap that becomes more pronounced from the point of Year 12 onwards. Attendance is considered a key reason for this disparity and is consequently a focus for future improvement in Indigenous education. Attendance matters for the obvious reason that, if you go to school, you might learn something. And if you do not reach and complete Year 7 or Year 8, your opportunities to become an autonomous learner will be limited.

A second 'known' is that younger people have better qualifications. According to the data, 15 to 35 year olds have better academic qualifications than the age groups above them. These findings defy the logic that suggests there was once a 'good old days' of Indigenous education that we should try to replicate. This is a myth: there is no such halcyon era to which we can return.

Further, we know that the more remote the area in which you live, the less chance you have of getting a decent education. Shockingly, only one-fifth of Indigenous people in remote locations have what we would all consider a basic education (Year 12 equivalent.)

We also know that, when it comes to the Indigenous population, if people do not have a decent education, they are not healthy. Nor does income seem to affect this correlation. Even people who benefit from what I call 'hyper welfare' conform to this trend. They might have a significant amount of money coming in by way of mining royalties; they might be able to buy a helicopter and new car every year; but they will still die of diabetes at 45, because there is a direct correlation between academic achievement and health.

One piece of good news is that, when it comes to labour market participation among holders of bachelor degrees, the Indigenous population outperforms the non-Indigenous population. That said, even if they hold a BA, Indigenous people still tend to smoke and drink more than their non-Indigenous colleagues, though this might be more a reflection on public service cultures, the chief employer of university-educated Indigenous Australians.

Efforts are being made to attract more Indigenous people to the private sector, with Western Australian mining magnate Andrew 'Twiggy' Forrest and former prime minister Kevin Rudd announcing in 2008 a project aimed at creating 50,000 Indigenous jobs as part of a so-called 'Australian Business Covenant'. In the Department of Education, we have set a target of about 900 additional employees, or 2.8 per cent of our workforce — the percentage of Australians who are Indigenous. This does not, however, reflect our actual client base (the number of Indigenous children in our schools, which is about 8 per cent). So we are a long way away from committing to having 8 per cent of our employees reflecting our student base.

The elephant in the room is the resources sector, and our potential to be an employer of choice for the Indigenous population. To date, what we are experiencing with our able and gifted Indigenous employees is that better money, conditions and, frankly, better jobs in the resources sector are drawing them away from public service. As a consequence, while we are trying to recruit more Indigenous people, we are doing so in a climate where there are other, preferred, employers.

I return now to my fundamental point: that the issue of Indigenous education is plagued by dichotomies. So, for example, the issue of school attendance tends to be expressed as a dichotomy — either a 'truancy model' or a 'connectedness model'.

Bluntly, truancy models do not work. It might make us feel good that we identify truants, lock them up and punish them, but the ramifications are usually counterproductive. One need only consider what happened in New South Wales, where models of truancy only succeeded in causing Indigenous students to attend less and be more criminalised.

The connectedness model develops on the pre-existing notion of inclusion of Indigenous people in Australian society. Yet, we must move beyond this agenda and shift the focus to *belonging*. To make Indigenous Australians belong, they need to first be connected. The connectedness model is built around the notion of the 'child at the centre' (CAC), in which users (in this case, children) are the central focus, with schools and communities wrapping around them accordingly. But how do we integrate the community into the decision-making processes? We are, I believe, beautifully placed and, in some ways, beautifully challenged, because we have a shopfront in every community — the principal and the school. So, we have invested in developing the kind of entrepreneurial leadership that would cut through bureaucratic impasses. When Tony Fitzgerald studied alcohol management in Cape York in 2001, one of the main recommendations he made was to suggest that a local champion (the director of nursing, the senior sergeant of police, or the school principal) should take a lead and formally coordinate government service delivery. To achieve this innovation is actually easier to do in small, remote communities than in the city context where principals have a disposition to consider their authority stopping at the school fence.

Whether it be alcohol management, welfare reform or remote community service provision, we are making significant inroads — albeit from a very low base. We are also seeing dramatic increases in participation at a community level. But above all, it is leadership that is required for citizen-centric advocacy for government service efficacy.

Finally, if we are to consider the difference between what is meant by 'engaged' and 'connected', we can see that the two are not interchangeable. Consider, for example, if we compare the statement, 'the child is not engaged' with 'the child is not connected'. While in the first instance the child is portrayed as the problem, in the second, it seems the child is being failed by their educator; the emphasis is on the educator being connected to the child, not the other way around. So we should ask: is the educator connected to the child's family and are they making decisions in the full knowledge of and in the interests of the child? And, bluntly, do our local educators know what they are doing and do they know what they stand for? In the final section, Michael Hansen will elaborate on this issue by looking at the case study of the school over which he presides, Cairns West State School.

Michael Hansen: One of our assistant directors-general always emphasised to principals the importance of teachers knowing the kids in their classes — knowing their data. As a practicing principal I need to know my own school, so that is where I will start.

Cairns West State School is a primary school in a low socio-economic area. In 2011 it had 600 pupils, 400 of whom were Indigenous. Only nine per cent of the students have English as a first language; the rest have it as their second language. Around 60 students are refugees and speak no English whatsoever. In the entire school, only four families — none of whom are Indigenous — have a mortgage. Perhaps 80 per cent of the parents are unemployed.

Other important statistics concern attendance and mobility. We enrolled 110 students in 2011. After the census date 75 left. That constitutes a huge mobility. If we do not address this issue we have a bigger problem, because those kids simply will not receive an education. As Australians, are we prepared to accept that as a given?

As well as knowing about the kids in my school, I also believe principals must know whom it is important to know. By this I mean that it is critical as a principal to be a people person. In my case, I have a clientele that, by and large, are very reluctant to engage with the system because, when they went to school, the system punished them. Consequently, it is vital that we become connected to our clients.

In a school like Cairns West, we need to be committed to doing our best for the pupils, but we also need to do more than that. In order to address the attendance issues we face, we need to also engage the parents. We have established that, if we continue the approach that educators have previously undertaken at schools like Cairns West, then we are only going to get more of the same. More of the same, for kids like that, is not good enough, because by and large these kids were failing.

Our new approach is what we call an 'academic success guarantee'. And what we guarantee is this: we will sign an agreement with the parents, not with the child, and the child can never be kicked off the program once the parents sign up to the agreement. The agreement we offer is that if parents send their children to school for 95 per cent of the time, then we will guarantee that they will meet or beat their year level benchmarks. No excuses. If an individual child does not meet the benchmarks, then they will be individually case-managed until such a time as they meet or beat those year level benchmarks.

We currently have over 200 students on this program. This means we have over 200 students who are attending 95 per cent of the time. And is it achieving demonstrable outcomes? It is. In 2008 only 32 per cent of the kids in our school reached minimum standards — not aspirational standards, just minimum standards. Last year we had 53 per cent of kids meeting minimum standards. We are not, in other words, even halfway through the journey of improving access for Indigenous pupils. Because, if these kids are not performing in school and they are not reaching minimum standards, then they are not going to be able to participate in society. That will merely serve to create another generation of welfare recipients.

Our parents are consumers like any other parent; except they do not have a lot of money. Most of them live day by day, from paycheck to paycheck, and often will send their kids to school because they have run out of money at home and have no food. But, like any parent, they want the best for their kids; I am yet to meet parents who do not want this. But, many of our parents do not know how to go about achieving the best. So, we have to market this idea of the 'academic success guarantee'.

Bearing this in mind, we went out into our community and said: 'If you keep your side of the bargain, we'll keep ours'. We cooked breakfasts, steaks, hamburgers and whatever it took to get them into school. And now, we get about 60 or 70 mums and dads who come in when we have our sign-up evenings, which take place every five weeks.

We are trying to give as many chances to the parents as possible. So, if some children only turn up, say, 60 per cent of the time for the first weeks (instead of 95 per cent), they would not qualify. But, after a few weeks of publicising the intention of the partnership, the kids are likely to turn up 95 per cent of the time. Their first five weeks are then wiped and they are now eligible for the program. They are given multiple chances over five week periods to improve attendance, and this message is reinforced at our regular big breakfasts.

Empowering the parents is a team effort. As a principal, my expectation is that our teachers, our teachers' aides and/or community members are out there working with the parents to help reach into the schools so that we can start to have conversations about improving their children's attendance rates.

While we undoubtedly have a long way to go to close the gap between Indigenous and non-Indigenous learning outcomes, the data for our program is encouraging. In fact, kids between Year 5 and Year 7 who are involved in our program are improving at a rate that is faster than the vast majority of schools in Australia. Of course, our kids start from a lower educational base. But you can imagine how it makes out parents feel when you show them, at a school-hosted big breakfast, for example, that because their kids are going to school, they are improving faster than any other children in Australia. It provides them with something they can go home and talk about and be proud of, because they are part of the partnership we have with them. Our agreement with the parents is that if we work together, then we can bridge the gap, or even overcome it.

Interestingly, at our school, we do not have a gap between Indigenous and non-Indigenous kids. In fact, often our Indigenous kids outperform the non-Indigenous kids. A gap remains, however, between our school's student cohort and the cohorts of the rest of state and of Australia.

Part of our 'academic success guarantee' is that every five weeks we collect data on the kids and we report back to parents on their improvements. We started doing this two-and-a-half years ago when we rolled out this program. This year, at the statewide principals conference, our director-general talked about the importance of regular data on performance. So, we like to think that, up in Cairns, we are leading the state agenda in this respect.

But the real story here is that closing the gap between Indigenous and non-Indigenous kids is a non-negotiable aim for governments at a state and federal level: it must be at the forefront of any policy for education. Because if we do not have that as our goal, whether it be me as principal of a school, or the director-general, or the minister, or the prime minister for that matter, then we are neither paying proper respect to the First Australians nor giving those kids, who are the descendants of those First Australians, an opportunity to participate in this wonderful country that we have.

Finally, as educators, how can we ensure that, were we to leave Cairns West State School, our partnership does not simply fall apart? Well, my responsibility is, and should be, that it is not a Michael Hansen-driven project: the implementation of this program is going to be an ongoing process. The program is going to be ingrained in the Cairns West culture. So, when anyone turns up at Cairns West State School, whether they are a parent, a replacement teacher or whether they come as the new principal, they have the 'academic success guarantee' to support them. Now other schools in our region are starting to embark on the journey that we have taken and, slowly but surely, the program will get down to Brisbane.

In conclusion, the traditional failures of schooling for Indigenous children in this country require that alternative approaches be implemented; chances must be taken. Undoubtedly, when we first came out with the 'academic success guarantee' model, it sounded like a harebrained idea. But, once we actually sat down and figured out the detail of the model, we had the confidence to take the risk of implementing this innovative approach. We had to put our feet on the ground and say: 'This is what we believe in. We have to do things differently.' And, because we dared to do things differently, we have now achieved a result that is starting to improve the education of our kids. That is why I turn up to work every single day — because those kids deserve more than my best; they deserve that I do whatever it takes so that, when they grow up, they can participate fully in society and their kids can become successful.

Part IV. Case Studies: Fostering community engagement and connectedness

14. Singapore's Social Safety Net and Human Service Provisions

Ang Bee Lian

Whatever model of human service provision they subscribe to, governments around the world face the dual challenges of an ageing population and rising expectations from their citizens. Globalisation has added a new twist to this challenge. In many parts of the world, free trade and open markets are blamed for widening income inequality and median wage stagnation. In more recent years, inflation of five per cent has negated any productivity gains and created a widening income gap.

Amidst this contemporary context, Singapore continues to pursue a policy of self-reliance-driven social inclusion. In Singapore, self-reliance is deemed to be the basis for a healthy work ethic; it allegedly drives private initiative and enterprise. Singapore's historical emphasis on economic development as a form of nation-building, coupled with a lack of government resources, has traditionally resulted in mutual help and a tendency to voluntarily contribute to the nation's development. This historically contributed to self-reliance, an attribute which is now considered a core Singaporean value to be preserved. (Not all will agree that the growth of the welfare state has been associated with an eroding work ethic, a deteriorating fiscal position and a growing entitlement mentality.)

So as needs and demand grow, and as Singapore is faced with the aforementioned contemporary challenges, how do we foster social inclusion while safeguarding the culture of self-reliance? This chapter is dedicated to answering this question. But first, consider the three pillars of Singapore's principle of social inclusion.

1. Subsidy in education

Subsided education is a key component of the Singaporean approach to social inclusion. As it is well known that education promotes social mobility, the Singaporean state creates equal opportunity through subsidising education, in the process attempting to avoid wide differences in educational opportunities according to socio-economic status. Singapore spends SGD$7000 (AUD$5300) per primary school student to ensure a high quality of education across the social spectrum and across all income groups, with generous subsidies also afforded to high school students. In this way Singapore's education system is the vehicle for a 'levelling up' effect. Ensuring social mobility, however, does not translate to ensuring equal outcomes because students are inherently different.

2. Home ownership

A second pillar of Singaporean social inclusion is the provision of housing that is affordable to the vast majority of the population. This is achieved through the Central Provident Fund (CPF), a centrally managed, compulsory pay-as-you-earn scheme. In addition to this, low-income families receive a state-sponsored grant to buy public housing flats, which themselves are subsidised and are purchased under the terms of a subsidised loan. These policies have been pursued in Singapore with the belief that housing is an appreciating asset that promotes social mobility, financial security and a sense of pride and belonging. In the 1960s, for example, a flat in the satellite town of Queenstown or Toa Payoh cost SGD$6200 (AUD$4700). By 1990, almost 90 per cent of Queenstown households owned their homes compared to 30 per cent in 1970. Moreover, the percentage of Queenstown households in one-to-three-room flats fell from 80 per cent in 1970 to 25 per cent in 2010. These figures indicate a gradual rise in the affordability of Singaporean housing.

3. Wage supplement to low-income workers

Faced with growing income inequality, Singapore has adopted a 'workfare' model instead of the traditional 'welfare' model. Under a traditional welfare approach, the state insures citizens against a range of risks, especially unemployment and illness. But, under a workfare approach, benefits are targeted at low-wage workers.[1] Tying government transfers to work avoids the moral hazard problems associated with unconditional transfers to the poor. The reason for this approach is that workfare could work better at redistributing incomes, while preserving the work ethic and promoting self-reliance. It covers nearly 20 per cent of the workforce, providing wage supplements of up to 20 per cent of the incomes of older, low-wage workers.

---

1   The Workfare Income Supplement scheme is adapted from the model originally introduced in Wisconsin, United States. See Jacqueline Poh, 'Workfare: The Fourth Pillar of Social Security in Singapore', in *Ethos*, 3 October 2007.

Challenges and trade-offs

The next part of this chapter will outline current challenges to Singapore's system of social inclusion. Some argue this model is too heavily geared towards housing, meaning less cash savings are allocated for retirement. Workfare payments, critics argue, can also result in reduced productivity by retaining more lower-skilled workers in the workforce than might otherwise have been the case. Another criticism is that Singapore's social safety nets are not sufficient — especially for the disabled, the aged destitute and the unemployable. Singapore is still seeking solutions to this issue that minimise the risk of unintended consequences. Moreover, if inflation is factored in and government aid factored out, how can we help vulnerable families advance to a lower-risk state of functioning? The challenge is to help these families to achieve progress.

A widening income disparity, an ageing population and the integration of foreigners (who are still viewed by some Singaporeans as a threat to their livelihood) are obvious issues with which Singaporean social policymakers have to deal. And, at the heart of the myriad challenges, is Singapore's unique approach to the social safety net — one woven out of the principles of personal and family responsibility. But, in an age when the institution of the family is under increasing stress, how long can Singapore hold on to the tenet that 'family is the first line of support'? The issues of what constitutes 'family' in the domain of human services continue to challenge those who administer assistance schemes; there is increasing pressure in Singapore to expand the definition of family to more accurately reflect contemporary social and demographic realities.

And what if some Singaporeans just cannot find work, even if they are able and willing to? The volatility of the new economy has led some experts to conclude that more workers could be unemployed for longer periods due to economic dislocation.

Workfare, an income supplement scheme, was introduced in 2007 and soon turned into a permanent social safety net. Other forms of relief range from housing grants to training and education subsidies. These schemes have helped make life a little easier for low-wage workers, by giving them more cash in hand, or opportunities to upgrade their skills for better jobs. Such a system would be rendered redundant if a growing number of Singaporeans cannot find work.

The impact of Singapore's pro-family policies and programs lies in the partnerships among state, private and community agencies, business and educational institutions and a network of social, cultural and religious organisations, in addressing the needs of families. The underlying social values, which may not be particularly 'Asian', such as the value of the family and community — the need to get one's house in order starting with the family and then the nation — provide the positive base for the social policy and programs. This model emphasises prevention and development, and provides a long-range perspective in dealing with problems which beset the family. It is an integrative approach rather than welfare or remedial in nature. It is empowering to the individual and the family and, in turn, instrumental in strengthening the social fabric of society.

Conclusion

Looking to the future, the main concern to the sustainability of the Singaporean approach is whether low-income earners or the unemployed perceive that they are advancing or improving their circumstances. In the longer term, we should be concerned whether inter-generational mobility can be improved, especially to ensure that low-income families do not remain in the 'poverty trap'. Singapore will continue to emphasise the education of its children and the upgrading of skills by its breadwinners as long-term strategies for the nation's families to achieve a better quality of life.

We in Singapore know that we cannot exclusively rely on market mechanisms. We need both good social policy and the market to work in tandem and in collaboration — a challenge that calls for calibration. As economist Amartya Sen puts it: 'the invisible hand of the market has often relied on the visible hand of government.'

Singapore's experience is that market principles are necessary to help government work better, and good government is necessary to help markets work better. This is not to suggest that Singapore has got the balance right; far from it — pragmatism and experimentation must continue.

The role of government is to work with the market. In order to effectively do this, the responsibilities of government may have to expand — to enable, regulate, stabilise and legitimise markets so that they can work better. Getting the balance right between markets and government will ultimately be the key to improving the standard of living and welfare of Singaporean citizens.

Appendix: Timeline of the development of Singapore's model of 'social inclusion'

1960s — Origins of social welfare and public assistance schemes; from 1968 workers were allowed to use their CPF savings to buy public housing. (Today, Singapore has one of the highest rates of home ownership among developed countries).

1970s — Focus on public housing and multiculturalism; government support for human services through provision of grants.

1980s — Focus on subsidised education as a vehicle for social mobility. From 1987 Singaporeans required to set aside a portion of their income in CPF until the age of 55 to provide them with a basic monthly income when they retire.

1990s — The 'Many Helping Hands' approach is initiated, whereby social services are provided by charities in a piecemeal manner. This decade also sees the start of the purchase of service or corporatist model of delivering human services, characterised by private and community partnerships.

2000s — Focus on governance and accountability; moving towards assistance for lowest 20 per cent of income-earners.

2010 — Reviews, re-engagement and renegotiation of the conditions of the social inclusion model.

15. Challenges in Engaging Citizens as Partners in the Community Sector

Yehudi Blacher

I am currently the Secretary of the Department of Planning and Community Development in Victoria, but have previously been associated with many state government agencies, including the Department of Premier and Cabinet, the Department of Human Services, and the Department for Victorian Communities.

My contribution to this volume primarily concerns the use of surveys as part of a process of citizen engagement. I will illustrate this by focusing on two surveys and, then, put them in the broader context of the range of engagement processes that my department undertakes.

I will begin, though, by setting some context for the department. The Victorian Department of Planning and Community Development was established in 2007 through the amalgamation of what was then the planning section in the Victorian government with the Department for Victorian Communities, which itself was established in 2002. Following the 2010 Victorian election, some of our responsibilities were transferred to other agencies, and other responsibilities were given to us. As a result we now have responsibility for the portfolios of land use planning, regional and community development, the regulation of local government, and sport and recreation, Aboriginal affairs, and veterans affairs. We have approximately 1000 staff, and we report to five ministers, the lead minister being the deputy premier.

The functions of our department have at their core the provision of support for the creation of strong, resilient, and effectively functioning communities. When the Department for Victorian Communities was established in 2002, it was the first time in Australia, and I think internationally, that there was a department created specifically for that purpose.

From the start we have been keen to engage directly with people in their communities about policy development and service delivery, and one of the ways we continue to do this is through surveys, but, over time, we have also utilised a large number of different engagement mechanisms. Apart from surveys, these have included regular community meetings, and new governance structures like regional management forums. Furthermore, in a structural sense, we have located our staff in communities to be direct conduits, brokers and facilitators between citizens, community organisations and government.

Let me now give two specific examples of our surveys. From the beginning, we recognised that the Department needed to gather real data on what people valued in their communities and on how well these aspirations were being met. In partnership with a number of government agencies we developed a set of indicators of community strength. These focused broadly on aspects relating to the creation of social networks, the degree of community participation, people's perceptions of safety in their own community, their ability to get help when needed, and local area amenity.

This data has now been collected in 10 annual, statewide surveys that form part of a broader Victorian population health survey, which is conducted by the Department of Human Services. Also, three surveys at a local government-area level were conducted in 2004, 2006, and 2008. Through the data obtained we have been able to understand the importance of: strong personal networks, how these networks generate benefits for both individuals and communities; governance in sustaining social capital; and, of course, the high value that people place on easy access to a range of community facilities.

One finding of our work, not surprisingly, is that different communities have different strengths and areas for improvement. This led the Department to introduce a range of programs that facilitated local communities' involvement in community planning and their subsequent access to investment opportunities through a number of grant programs funded by the Department and other agencies.

Caroline Springs, on the outskirts of Melbourne, is a region in which the department has undertaken particular work. There, we established a partnership between the government, the local shire (Melton Shire), and a developer (Delfin Lend Lease) to ensure the timely delivery of community infrastructure and its joint use. Throughout this process we gained a sense of what that partnership could mean for the cohesiveness and strength of the local community.

The project had well-designed performance indicators, and community surveys of the partnership — which were undertaken in 2005 and again in 2007 — represented another way of monitoring the efficacy of the partnership. The surveys showed significant improvement in relation to the performance indicators. Over time we saw an increase in attendance at community events, improved access to facilities and services, and a clear view that Caroline Springs was an active community — albeit a new one — where people got involved in local issues.

Compared with other places with similar demographics, more people in Caroline Springs experienced their community as a friendly and helpful one, and believed it to be a special place in which to live, and that there were opportunities for people to have a say and to get involved. These indicators of community satisfaction are now widely used by a range of Victorian government departments, by local governments in their council plans, and by a range of other community based organisations.

And yet, in our role of overseeing local government, we are aware of the potential confusion arising from overlapping roles and responsibilities between the various tiers of government. Two issues — the division of responsibility between state and local government and the responsibility of elected members to effectively raise revenue — raise existential questions about our system of government.

That said, in Victoria in the 1990s, when there was a strong regime of rate-capping in place following reforms to local government, the prevailing mood was that it was a very blunt tool. Certainly, the councils proclaimed that it did not effectively enable them to transfer risk for underinvestment to the state government, because the state government was stopping them raising appropriate levels of revenue.

When that restraint was taken off, over the last 10 years or so, what we have seen is local government rates increase at a level that is probably three or four percentage points a year above the rate of inflation. This is an issue that concerned the previous Labor government under John Brumby, and it is one that will become a concern for the current Coalition government under Ted Baillieu.

It is interesting that we are only now beginning to detect community resistance to rate increases and, even though we have had the data for some time, there has previously not been a concerted attempt to explore this. It is likely that, over time, the Baillieu government will attempt it, by meshing the satisfaction data with the rate increase data.

I maintain a pragmatic approach to resourcing questions. There are issues about the responsibility of councillors to set their own level of resourcing. And council rates, which can form a significant part of any council's budget, are taxes that many residents simply pay year-on-year. Unless there are pressures from other sources, these amounts do creep up. For example, rates have increased at a much faster rate than the cost of gas and electricity over that period of time, and yet the cost of utilities seems to be at the forefront of public debate, whilst rate increases have not been.

In 2002, the Steve Bracks Labor government brought out an overarching strategic framework called *Growing Victoria Together*, and a number of our indicators were selected as measures of progress against one of the core objectives, which was building cohesive communities. The indicators were also instrumental in shaping the previous government's social policy framework called *A Fairer Victoria*, from its inception in 2005 through to 2010. Through the measures which were constantly surveyed over that period of time, the government was able to see an increase in general community satisfaction with the level of community infrastructure provided, the level of satisfaction rising from 80 per cent in 2006 to 85 per cent in 2008.

The *A Fairer Victoria* framework caused a decline in the proportion of Victorians who were members of a group in their local communities, albeit a relatively small decline. I think this decline largely reflects both national and international trends but, interestingly, we saw an increased proportion across the state of people who believed that they had an opportunity to have a say in matters affecting them. Between 2005 and 2010 this percentage increased from 36 per cent to 42 per cent — even though this is still a low figure.

In summary, the indicators have provided a guide for community planning and action to address local issues, a rationale for government intervention to improve connections in local communities, and an ongoing way, over that period from 2005 to 2010, of measuring whether those interventions were effective.

Let me now turn to my second example, which is an annual community satisfaction survey of local government performance. This has been the responsibility of our local government division since the surveys began in the late 1990s. Initially funded by the Victorian state government, the esteem in which local councils now hold these surveys is reflected in the fact that they now fully fund it. The Department continues, however, to oversee its production, conduct the analysis of the results, and release information publically.

A minimum of 350 telephone interviews are conducted in each municipality, resulting therefore in 28,000 interviews across the state, which in turn provides some insightful feedback. The Victorian Population Health Survey, to which I referred earlier, actually conducts 450 interviews per local government authority, which increases the number of interviews conducted statewide to over 30,000.

Respondents to the council survey are asked questions to determine their level of satisfaction with the performance of their councils across a whole range of service areas, including their advocacy role, customer contact and community engagement, as well as assessing the council's overall performance. A statewide research result summary, 'Local Government in Victoria', is published annually. This provides average performances for all the councils, and comparative results for five groups of councils, inner and outer metropolitan councils, rural cities and regional centres, and large and small shires. Individual reports are also provided for each council on their own performance.

This survey has allowed us to measure the performance of council's in Victoria over time. Since 1998 we have seen an improvement of eight percentage points in the percentage of respondents who rate their councils as excellent, good, and adequate, from (69 to 77 per cent). And it also tells us how they are performing in particular activities. For example, the 2011 results revealed that residents thought their councils do reasonably well in delivering health and human services. In fact, a staggering 89 per cent think they perform well in that area, and in the area of recreational facilities, 81 per cent. This sentiment was not shared when residents were asked about how well their council was maintaining their local roads and footpaths. And it is disappointing to note that, generally, satisfaction with the broader role of councils in community engagement has declined from in the mid 1970s, in the early years of the survey, to 67 per cent this year.

But the survey does provide rich data for state government, local councils and, of course, residents. It enabled councils to communicate their achievements to their community, and to compare their performance against other councils. And I cannot emphasise enough the importance of that comparative opportunity: councils always look one across the other, and are sensitive about their performance as compared with a similar cohort.

It also provides state government with data to assess council performance and trends over time, and identify whether regulatory or policy intervention might be required. And, perhaps most importantly, it provides residents with information that they can use to lobby for service improvements, or indeed change their elected representatives.

Surveys are one way of collating the data and establish the evidence about what communities need and value. The surveys we do, the data we provide, and the community engagement processes we undertake are the tools we use to: try to understand what people think and want; to identify how government policies, programs, and systems are working; and to provide input into policy development and service and system improvements.

These engagement tools fall into four categories. Firstly, the gathering of the evidence through surveys and research (and I cannot emphasise enough the importance of the factor of time in conducting the surveys and collating the responses). The local government survey has been taking place for 12 years, and there is, as a result, a rich source of data to draw upon. The surveys that we have done in relation to the first set of indicators have, in various forms, been going on now for close to nine years.

Second is the act of taking the department into the community, through the work that departmental staff do in local communities, performing a brokering and facilitating role, and encouraging the formation of partnerships between local organisations, councils, and residents.

Third is the provision of opportunities for members of the community to be engaged should they wish to be. This is done through forums, such as our regular community meetings, where senior departmental staff meet directly with the local community. As these are openly structured meetings, anybody who wants to come is welcome. Such occasions enable us to hear directly, unmediated by others, the views and experiences of people.

While the planning systems vary from state to state, I think one of the characteristics of them across the country is the formal process that one must go through to comment on changes to planning schemes, or the possibility of particular sorts of development. They are rigid and inflexible and generally lack transparency.

If I had a particular wish, it would be to embed into the Victorian planning system a range of requirements for councils to be more open and engaging, and to do this at the front end, when they are amending planning schemes, rather than to do it through a relatively passive advertising process. I believe that, over time, this would encourage more people to have their say.

And yet, active citizen engagement is not a hallmark of Australia's political and civic culture; the prevailing assumption that people do not want to get involved in the political and civic process ought to be interrogated.

Finally, our fourth engagement tool is a substantial investment in capacity building. This involves supporting community members to obtain the necessary skills to participate in community organisations. To me, these different types of engagements are essential elements of what good public administration is about. But I often reflect on how rarely these elements are seen as core activities of government agencies.

There is, however, always room for improvement. The next five years will see variation in our focus on the intensive face-to-face engagement that has dominated the Department's recent connection with community. The increased use of social media has the potential to allow us to continue this work; other Victorian agencies are already maximising its potential.

16. Challenges in Engaging Citizens as Partners in Housing

Shane Chisholm

I have a background in and a passion for frontline engagement with citizens, so my contribution to this volume is operationally focused. Since 2009, I have been the Customer Service Manager for the Housing New Zealand Corporation. In this role I am responsible for the development of a national strategy and associated program of work to enhance the customer service provided by the Housing New Zealand Corporation. The program is focused on increasing the levels of both internal and external customer satisfaction.

First though, what is the Housing New Zealand Corporation? As New Zealand has a long and proud history of serving its communities and meeting their housing needs, our mission statement is simple and clear: it is to help New Zealanders in their time of housing need. Our chief focuses are the identification of priority housing needs, the provision of appropriate housing solutions, and the provision of ongoing support to enable our customers a greater degree of independence. We also manage the Crown's social housing and resources, and we are obliged to do that efficiently.

We currently support over 200,000 customers through the provision of a number of housing-related products and services; our primary service is the 68,000 state-owned properties that are distributed throughout New Zealand. We have a wide and varied customer base.

The Customer First program, which is the focus of this essay, is one of a number of operationally focused programs that contributed to the Housing New Zealand Corporation's initial tranche of change. This transformative journey includes refreshing our information and communications technology (ICT) platform, introducing new finance systems and customer relationship management systems, and reconfiguring our service delivery model throughout New Zealand. The exciting thing about this is that, at the heart of the transformation, is a desire to become more customer-centric.

The Customer First strategy and initial work program was endorsed by Housing New Zealand's executive team in September 2009. The primary objective of the program was to initiate a process of change, to bring the customer to the forefront and, by doing so, identify opportunities to effect positive change in relation to the customer service experience.

In saying that, however, there were three very simple goals established for this program. The first and most important goal was customer voice — to listen, to understand, and to respond appropriately to our customers. This goal was our initial focus, and it has influenced the activities and outcomes of the following two goals.

The second goal — customer focus — is about creating a service culture that encourages and enables our staff to deliver a customer service experience that meets and sometimes exceeds our customers' expectations. And the third goal is focused on customer choice, ensuring that Housing New Zealand has accessible, relevant, and user-friendly products and services.

In relation to the first goal, improving customer voice, there were three key areas on which it was necessary to focus. First, we had to review and align our existing quantitative and qualitative customer research, particularly customer satisfaction surveys. Second, we had to effectively manage complaints and compliments. Third, we had to better utilise the rich data that we had about our customers to better understand both the current and future customer profile.

Housing New Zealand had a number of existing customer satisfaction measurement activities and surveys, each operated in isolation of the other. We sought to consolidate these survey activities in order to ensure that we obtained an appropriate representation of all our customers. As a part of this consolidation activity we introduced the Kiwi's Count Common Measurement Tool. This is a concise and validated set of statements and questions that reflect our key customer satisfaction drivers. These measures are owned and used right across government in New Zealand, and across different government agencies.

We introduced transparent quarterly reporting across all channels. The results were published to all areas, for all areas. This promoted healthy discussion and sharing of best practice, enabling managers across the corporation to understand what was working well, what was not, and how they could collaborate to address problems.

The key to the customer satisfaction surveys and driving reform was that the satisfaction survey results became a core performance measure for the Corporation, automatically focusing our staff's attention on ensuring those results came through. The intelligence extracted from this research has informed future change; it has pointed us in the right direction by identifying the 'pain points' for our customers, and has exposed things that the Corporation was reluctant to acknowledge.

The surveys provide us with good, clear direction. There are a number of other activities, such as focus groups, that the Corporation undertakes to identify the fundamental issues. But, that satisfaction levels have increased over time suggests that the information we are receiving, and the action we are taking, is having a positive impact on our customers.

The ability to share results and best practice — not only across the Corporation but also across agencies via the common measurement tool — has been a valuable experience. There have, however, been challenges, including acceptance of the common measurement tool as being relevant to assessing the type of customer encountered by Housing New Zealand. Our research and evaluation team reconfirmed, however, that there was a strong alignment between the previously completed research and these common measurement tools. Sharing our performance results was also, initially, a challenge for us as there was some reluctance to reveal progress.

We have also re-engineered how we manage and respond to complaints and compliments from our customers. Accessibility was a key to achieving this. Prior to this process of change, the only way a customer of the Corporation could register a complaint was in writing. To allow us to access this valuable information, it was essential that the complaints process was simplified. The benefit derived from this process was the opportunity that this feedback provided to learn from our mistakes, and to address the root cause of the issues. We are still working on that today.

The third area of focus is in relation to customer intelligence and, in particular, we focused on customer segmentation in order to understand the profile of both our current and future customers. This is a complex and long-term project.

As for our second goal — concerning our service culture — Housing New Zealand last year published its 'customer promise'. This represents a contract between Housing New Zealand and its customers that sets clear guidelines about the behavioural expectations of each party. It is based on our key customer satisfaction drivers, and therefore some level of our performance can now be measured from the customer satisfaction survey results.

Our customer promise is communicated proactively and regularly to our customers and this upfront investment in communication is fundamental. We spend time with our customers when they first engage with us through the customer promise process, and this has paid substantial dividends in the ongoing and long-term relationships that we have.

The promise comprises six statements about what the customer can expect from Housing New Zealand staff, and four statements in relation to how Housing New Zealand expects our customers to respond. This has been one of the most effective tools that we have used to change the culture — both internally and externally with the customer — of our customer service.

We are also finding that our internal shared service partners are using the same promise to measure their own success with regard to engagement in the internal services they deliver to other areas within the organisation.

As well as the launch of the customer promise, there was a need to equip staff with understanding, knowledge, and tools to deliver on this promise. Consequently, the Service Excellence Training program was developed and delivered nationwide, providing staff with service standard guidelines on how to engage with our customers.

When we launched the customer promise, were we confident that we could deliver on it? The answer is no. But we were committed to improvement and progress, and that was the key.

To conclude, everything that Housing New Zealand learned from the Customer First program — a simple grassroots operational program — stems from listening to the customer. The volume of information that we have at our fingertips — even without engaging our customer — was phenomenal, and the need for us to use that information to improve our service was evident. The valuable lessons learned include the need to 'keep it simple', to adapt process to meet needs and to undertake due diligence without impeding action. It is crucial to have strong, positive leadership in this area. Finally, internally, it is all about positioning — to recognise and celebrate achievement, and encourage and support a teamwork environment.

17. Building Citizen Feedback into Program Redesign

James Mowat, Jim Scully and David Sweeney

James Mowat: In my contribution to this chapter I will discuss how a problematic institution for stakeholders and customers was turned, in the early 2000s, into what is today considered a model in the field of government regulation in New Zealand — Land Information New Zealand (LINZ). I will outline what the problems with LINZ were, how they were addressed through the involvement of customers and stakeholders and, finally, list the lessons learnt through this process. First, though, I will provide some context about what we do.

LINZ manages eight per cent of New Zealand's land, three million hectares of Crown land including the South Island high country — some of the most spectacular scenery in the world. Our mandate from government is to manage information about land, manage transactions concerning land, and manage land on behalf of the Crown. This mandate comprises five functions: regulatory, to enable trade and commerce involving designated lands; land title, to help inform people of their property rights and those of others; surveying, to establish property boundaries; valuation, to enable landholders to know how much their properties are worth; and, finally, Crown land, to inform citizens how public land is put to its best use or what happens if the Crown needs to acquire private land for public works.

In 2004, LINZ was widely criticised and accused of having regulations that were inconsistent and not fit for purpose. This criticism stemmed from the fact rules, standards and guidelines were written in the backroom and then put into the public sphere; in other words, we would tell people to comply with rules, without seeking input from the public. This approach was frustrating for those whose circumstances made it necessary for them to interact with LINZ. They felt they did not know what they needed to do to comply with our rules and regulations, and they wanted to perform their roles with a clear sense of direction. Something had to change.

In 2004 LINZ did not have expert knowledge of the practices captured in our process, so the starting point for reform was to form a new regulatory group that was split from the operations side of the business and, in the first instance, to perform a stocktake of all our regulatory documentation. The review found that LINZ had over 300 different documents administering our practices, including differing standards, guidelines, specifications, fact sheets, rules, guidance notes and operation material. There was no common approach or philosophy about how land management was to be regulated; consequently, the regulators operated in isolation from each other.

Prior to 2004, LINZ had not consulted the regulated community about what they knew and how things happened at the coalface. It was clear that we needed to move to performance-based regulation, to talk and engage with the regulated community, and to strip out that operational material. The 'optimal regulation' approach was taken; using as little as possible, and as much as necessary to produce efficient services. LINZ adopted a philosophy that was similar to many other service provision re-engineering exercises in that it advocating the merits of 'light-handed regulation' or 'less red tape'. We certainly knew that we needed a new set of traffic lights for our customers.

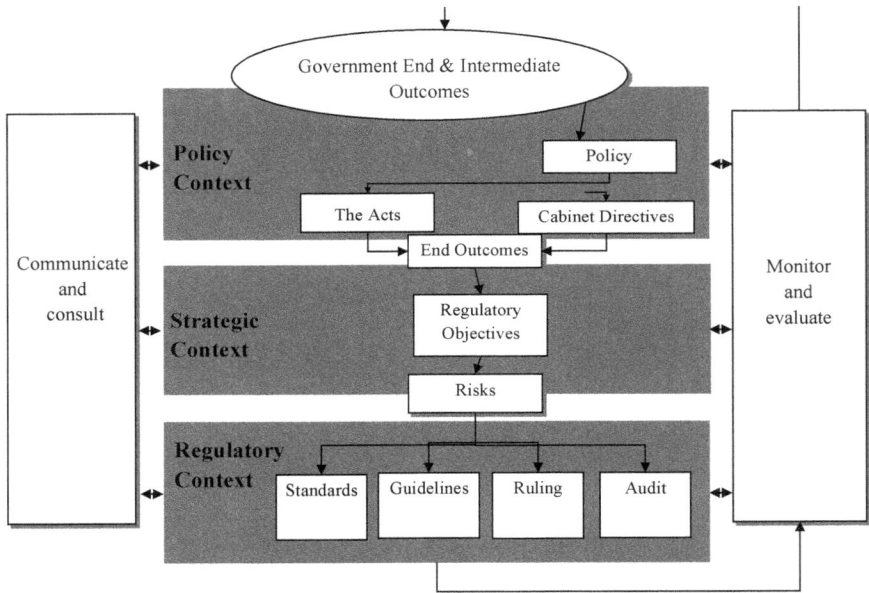

Figure 1: LINZ strategic context

Source: Land Information New Zealand.

At the top of Figure 1 is what government requires from us to enforce its legislation related to land trade and commerce; the bottom depicts the way in which LINZ operated in the past. Previously, we examined the legislation and then wrote our standards, guidelines, and rulings, and audited against these regulations. But we found there was a significant gap in the middle, the 'strategic context' — which is the gap where the regulators need to develop their own outcomes and objectives in the context of the aims of the legislation. Doing this made it much easier for LINZ to move between the top and the bottom.

This much clearer expression of our outcomes represented both the clarification of a major linkage between the legislative branch and LINZ. Our next step was to establish a dedicated regulatory standards team who would own and manage the frameworks and processes. This team administers a risk framework to determine the regulatory needs; ultimately, they decide whether to intervene or not. As well as developing and maintaining a toolkit for the regulators, the team members also act as project managers, helping to develop new interventions. They provide expert advice on drafting technical content and they remain more neutral than the regulator in challenging their thinking and logic. We have followed both New Zealand and international examples of organisational approach to develop standards that are used by our expert committee and in our public consultation processes. This team also ensures that our published documents have a consistent look and feel.

After the separation of the regulatory from the operational functions, our regulatory group would lend its four principal regulators, including the registrar-general of land and the surveyor-general, to the operational group. These officials are responsible for providing the technical expertise from their regulatory area. The regulatory group can then review existing regulatory documents and decide what level of regulation is needed so that, if there is a high risk, they can choose to apply the appropriate rule or a standard without a mandate. If there is lower risk involved, then they will use guidelines for best practice. The regulatory group maintains overall responsibility for the content and eventual approval of all regulatory determinations.

In addition to the deliberate split between the operation side of LINZ and the creation of a new regulatory group, we also faced the challenge of changing our behaviour. We decided to no longer draft completed regulatory documents and then simply hand them out at that stage. Our 'frameworks and processes team' recognised that we needed to involve and educate our external stakeholders. For a while, some of those regulated still said: 'We want prescriptive regulation. Just tell us how to do it and we'll do it'. But it was clear that the engagement and support of that community which we regulate required fostering so, instead, we adopted an external expert committee procedure to assist with our decision-making. This gave us a formal way to tap into the knowledge of our practitioners, facilitated by workshops and emails to debate and resolve the content of the new standards. These experts gave their time and resources willingly to assist what they knew, particularly with their involvement, would be a better product.

When expert committees were created, they shared the responsibility for developing a satisfactory outcome from the regulated communities. In fact, the experts were eager to tell us when our regulations were not good enough, and were keen to be involved in the improvement of the system. In this way, customers are accessed through the experts, who act as their proxies. For example, if you are buying or selling a house and you register with us, then you need to use a solicitor; the solicitor in that case is an expert who gives us feedback. The same is true of surveyors and valuers. We found it beneficial to bring these experts in to talk to us. One thing we haven't done, though, is gone out to survey the public to see whether the experts are telling us anything that the public do not want done.

Once the expert committee had finalised and approved a draft standard we moved to the public consultation phase. To assist us, we entrusted the help of a senior law enforcement officer, who had previously embarked on an internet-based public consultation process concerning New Zealand's new *Summary Offences Act*. He recalled that seeking feedback from former clients of criminal regulation was unhelpful — so we were forewarned that seeking client input might be problematic. When it came to our public consultation process, we also used a website and email distribution list to attract as wide a range of feedback as possible, and continue to use this medium. For example, when reviewing leased properties in the South Island high country, we sought and received feedback from a range of NGOs, such as environmental groups interested in the forests, birds, fish, game, and public access rights. Unlike the consultation over the changes to criminal law, we received a wealth of good feedback from our experts and users in the regulated community. In addition, the banking sector and police provided invaluable advice on identity theft for the creation of a standard on transacting land in order to minimise the risk of fraudulent property transfers. When required by law we advertise in public newspapers, but we have found our best source of feedback to be via the internet, as this is the medium of communication with the widest reach.

Overall, the results of the LINZ approach to developing regulatory standards have been overwhelmingly positive. The regulated communities with which we work have taken part in developing our new documents. They have given positive feedback about the process, particularly the committee meetings for experts who provide significant input to make effective standards that are then accepted by the regulated community. The documents produced met our quality criteria; we have had this verified by external consultants, and the new standard documents are now fit for purpose.

We have reduced the number of regulatory documents from 300 to 55, and we now know why we intervene when we do — the strong supporting rationale based on risk assessment provides the justification. Working through the process of change has been hard work; it took much longer than we planned and a huge amount of energy, drive and resilience. On the completion of the program redesign, Malcolm Sparrow, professor of practice of public management at Harvard University, commented that, faced with a similar reform agenda, most agencies would have given up long ago. We have been left with a consistent approach to regulation across the regulatory group and buy-in from the rest of the organisation and our external partners.

And yet, as an organisation with both a regulatory side and an operation side, in the early days of reform we struggled to get the organisation to sing from the same song sheet. In fact, a lot of the resistance we got early on was from the operations side, which expressed disatisfaction with what was perceived to be overly prescriptive regulations. Some of our biggest battles were internal and this problem needed to be addressed before we engaged with external stakeholders. Once we had learnt this lesson, we made sure that we got everyone within the organisation on side and then we began to engage with external stakeholders.

In conclusion, the ultimate lesson we learnt from this process is that planning is vital; nothing happens without first getting the right building blocks in place. We also learnt that we needed good management and realistic timeframes; that we needed internal agreement before moving to the external regulated community; that we needed to be flexible and innovative throughout the reform process; that we needed a champion at senior management level to support and maintain momentum throughout the process; and finally, that we had to adhere to good process and be prepared to defend it. This is not always easy, as the expert committee and public consultation phases consume significant time and resources, meaning many critics want to cut resources to save time and money.

But, ultimately, the reforms enacted by LINZ since 2004 have been a success. Today, the New Zealand Government is challenging all of the country's public agencies to be less regulatory in their orientation; in LINZ we are pleased to be through to the other side with a clear sense of direction about how we can best deliver our services.

Jim Scully: While earlier in this volume Christian Bason focused on the technology and government side of service provision, in my contribution I will focus on the customer side — a pertinent subject given the natural disasters that occurred in 2011 in Queensland, Christchurch and Japan. I would like to draw on the observations of Patrick Whitney of the Illinois Institute of Technology, who talks of an 'innovation gap' where customer services are concerned (see LaConte 2007). Whitney argues that, when it comes to service delivery, while we have become technologically and operationally proficient, we have become less empathetic in understanding the customer's world. There is consequently an empathy gap concerning what is desirable to end users. Whitney argues that, if we understand this and draw insights from it, then this is what really drives innovation.

In his contribution to this chapter, Mowat discusses regulations shaping policy and the need to maintain the integrity of the system. I will devote my comments to highlighting examples where policy has been translated into administration; following me in this chapter, David Sweeney will expand on this theme and discuss the ability of administrators to stay true to their intent as they go through this transformation process.

We often speak of technology driving us forward; and we apply our minds to what's viable from a business point of view. When I worked for Telecom, we spent a lot of time considering these two issues. Next we thought about citizens, customers, the end user and the notion of 'balance breakthrough'. Elsewhere in this volume, contributors write of the need to start thinking about the citizen, the customer and the user up-front, as experts or insiders, it becomes critical to imagine seeing the world from an outsider's perspective.

There's also the idea of pathways and customer journeys; in fact Richard Buchanan talks about systems being so complex that you do not actually experience them, you only experience your pathway through one particular system (Buchanan 2010). And while we, as insiders, think of these customer pathways as being easy to navigate, the outsider's reality can be very different.

For example, while working at New Zealand Inland Revenue, the language used was of customer segmentation: we had 'students', we had 'individual taxpayers' and we had 'families'. Yet, the reality is, when you stand in another person's world, it rarely falls so easily into these stark categories. A customer, for example, could both have a student loan, have started a small business, and have participated in New Zealand's voluntary long-term saving scheme, KiwiSaver. In other words, any one person may have a mixed and fragmented customer profile, yet, when they need a particular service, they have multiple channels coming at them which may not suit their needs or alignment.

Overly complex messages and frequent changes for consumers are also to be avoided if we are to meet better their needs. In Inland Revenue we went out to small-to-medium businesses and offered to assist them in managing their affairs. The overwhelming response from these clients was to leave them alone. Every time we introduced a new improvement, they had to change their business systems. Such tinkering with a particular system meant that every time we enacted a change, clients had to go through a re-learning process, which was not always successful. To illustrate this, one day we spoke to a business about the range and comprehensiveness of our written communication with firms. A representative of that business told us he was thrilled with our level of communication, because he was using all our paperwork to light his fire at home. It's a true story.

Nor do we think that we should seek citizen feedback only when restructuring is necessary. To best engage with the public, citizen feedback must be a built-in feature; it must be a continuous loop. In fact, in New Zealand, the smartest government departments are using websites, iPhone apps, Android apps and social media in order to keep this feedback coming in. And yet, this is not simply a matter of technology. It is one thing for an organisation to adhere to the principal of engagement and contribution, but quite another to make them comfortable with listening to and taking on such feedback. This is often one of the most pressing concerns for organisations.

In the last third of this chapter, David Sweeney will discuss, from the perspective of the Australian Commonwealth Department of Human Services, the issue of incorporating customers' voices into policy changes.

David Sweeney: To round off this chapter exploring citizen input into program design, I will discuss the work that we at the Department of Human Services have done in establishing our method for understanding customer journeys as a way of advancing the department's service delivery reform agenda. So far we have prototyped this method by using a representative from five different customer groups: a new parent, a recently separated adult, a single mother, a male approaching retirement, a father of one and a person experiencing homelessness. The process entailed three stages. The first stage was about discovery and exploration — the research stage. We next moved into the synthesis and analysis stage that Bason has written about (in Chapter 5 of this volume). We concluded with a mapping and a visualisation stage.

Before I elaborate on the different stages of this process, though, let me say that in my home country, the United Kingdom, where effects of the global financial crisis continue to be felt and the public sector is bearing much of the brunt of those economic cutbacks, I believe the tendency to redesign services with an emphasis on public participation has increased, not lessened. This, I think, is because people have realised that we need to think about the way in which we deliver services differently and so we need to not only find efficiencies, but also consult the general public — the service users — about where the cuts are going to happen and what impact that is going to have on people. By involving customers in the redesign of service delivery, we can bring new ideas into the system that perhaps would not otherwise be appearing in what is, after all, an economically constrained environment.

I will now explain the different stages of the aforementioned customer journey process. Firstly, the discovery stage essentially involved us going out and talking to customer groups firsthand in a location of their choice — often in their own homes. During these consultations our goal was to understand what the journey is like for our customers. We did not have any preconceived expectations about their customer service experience; rather, we simply listened to them describe it.

We wanted to gain insights from their journeys and this required us to approach our clients with an open mind; we tried to uncover their needs and to understand their emotions, motivations and ambitions in order to get to the synthesis and visualisation stages. The synthesis stage began while we were collecting the data; we would collect the data — often in teams of two or three — and then debrief our office from the field. This approach enabled us to return to the office and rapidly gather the data together, looking for common themes and creating appropriate aggregated visualisations of a number of different journeys. In total, we talked to well over 30 people, so these maps are an aggregate of several different people's stories.

The homelessness journey was important to us because those interviewed had compelling stories to tell about their experiences on the streets. We spoke to those who were currently homeless about their goals, needs, who is involved in their lives and how they think they will break the homelessness cycle. We found that they often get trapped and that they face not only the issue of finding housing but also of employment.

Even without asking them about their interactions with government, the respondents told us about this subject quite freely. The stories often shockingly illustrated the way homelessness support services at state and federal levels frequently do not align. And, while we didn't set out to ask the respondents if they had solutions to their problems, in some cases they volunteered them, which we then attempted to factor into our visualisations accordingly. Their criticisms of state and federal service providers often included statements such as: 'I don't understand why you're not doing this', or 'wouldn't it be better if you were doing that'?

So, we have collected suggestions, criticisms and proposed solutions; they will undoubtedly be more valuable further down the track as we revise our programs. For example, one of the things we need to do is to validate some of these journeys; we need to go back to these customers to ask if we have correctly rendered their journey in our visualisations. After this process of verification and validation we will invite the interview respondents to discuss ways of improving our system.

We are still prototyping this work and thinking about other ways of improving upon it. In particular, we are looking at how we can take these visualisations and make them meaningful for people who are creating mechanisms to improve experiences and outcomes for customers.

References

Buchanan, R. 2010. 'Design for Service', Keynote address at the Savannah College of Art and Design, 9th October.

LaConte, V. 2007. 'Innovation by Design', *Illinois Institute of Technology Magazine*, Illinois, Winter.

18. New Ways of Engaging Citizens in Service Delivery

Nicole Pietrucha and Jo Sammut

Nicole Pietrucha: Much of this volume concerns engaging citizens through notions such as co-design and co-design practice. But, how do we actually build those frameworks and how do we think about this on the ground as a real practice? In my contribution I will attempt to answer some of these questions in relation to the work we are doing in the Commonwealth Department of Human Services (DHS) about building co-design capability.

First though, I need to stress the fact that this work is in its infant stages. We started our project around June 2010, so, in fact, many of the questions readers may have concerning co-design I cannot yet answer in relation to our own project, because we are yet to fully test and implement it. Indeed, as with many in this field, we are still grappling with questions concerning whether co-design works, and how to approach issues associated in the future.

Before such issues can be explored, some context is required. The co-design project is part of a broader initiative that is happening in the portfolio on service delivery reform, and there are close to 20 large associated projects, one of which concerns co-design.

This project draws upon an already strong tradition of engagement that exists in the department; of working with stakeholders and of having relationships at a local level. But, the challenge for me and the people that work with me in DHS, has been how to rectify existing engagement processes that had developed badly: how would we incorporate more community input into policy processes to create effective co-design; what are the tools and techniques we need to introduce into the portfolio to support that work?

In the initial stages of this project we have been focusing on identifying the core framework that the portfolio needs to improve engagement and to develop policy co-design capability. In essence, the aim is to involve users and the community in designing improved service delivery through building a co-design capability. This is part the everyday work that is done in the portfolio and of a broader service delivery reform program. It is also part of another major initiative in the portfolio about participation measures that was announced in May 2011.

The first challenge has been to define what we mean by 'co-design'. As a current buzzword, people use it liberally and to describe a whole range of things. Consequently, it risks being falsely interchanged with other terms concerning community engagement, and concerning how we work with community.

At Medicare, however, our understanding of co-design is that it matches collaborative participation and design thinking with users, customers and stakeholder staff. By design thinking, I refer to those specific concepts and approaches that Christian Bason broaches in Chapter 5.

According to this thinking, collaborative participation involves challenging ourselves to work with customers and the community; it involves challenging ourselves to ask individuals about their own circumstances and human experiences. And, we think that engagement and participation should start as early as possible in the relationship.

While it may be easy to consult the public when general directions have been set, what is not easy is undertaking the observation work that Bason discussed, and using that to inform new strategic directions. As Lynelle Briggs points out (Chapter 7), this process also has the potential to inform policy thinking about broader agendas.

These are the issues with which DHS has been grappling. For DHS, co-design will be about blending design thinking with participation, with the expectation of improving customer experience.

As a portfolio, DHS wants to get feedback about what does and does not work on the ground, and to use that to shape our approach to design new services and work with the community.

DHS has a vision about what might be the best model for the portfolio. The techniques and tools that we currently use to engage with our customers include the 29 community forums that we have so far conducted. These were traditional community forums where we gathered groups together to have conversations about their views on service delivery. Their accounts of their customer service experience with DHS and their suggestions for improvements were the starting points for developing our co-design capability.

Our future goal is to build co-design capability to include customers, staff and stakeholders, potentially in the exploration phase (focusing on the issues we are facing in the portfolio) and then in the innovation phase (focusing on how we would prototype new co-design models and make them available for testing so as to evaluate their readiness for use in the creation of new services and programs).

The past year has been spent in determining the model and methodology that we might need. We have also been looking at ways of harnessing customer insight. A live action project has started in Victoria, which involves conducting community engagement through our customer service officers and the relevant local municipal association in order consult with particular communities about issues that they face.

We have developed some guiding principles on the governance of our organisation with which staff will become familiar. In an organisation of over 40,000 people, it is fundamental to have a clear set of guiding principles so that our staff can be confident of the reform they are enacting in developing this new co-design model.

For the model itself, co-design will be applied both at the strategic part of the journey (thinking about what new ideas and strategic directions we are pursuing) and at the service design part of the process (harnessing some of the design techniques and practices discussed by Bason to refine particular projects or programs).

For us, co-design is the engine prototyping the application of design techniques; co-design allows rapid development, testing and evaluation that can be used to inform new projects and programs.

The idea is that co-design work — in which DHS works directly with its customers — is undertaken within a framework that makes the possible and viable clear. Customers have valuable expertise to offer to us about how new services and programs will impact on them, and they are well-placed to appraise performance once those services and programs are rolled out.

In addition to the broad community research conducted in 2010, Medicare has worked to improve service delivery by mapping a series of customer journeys to further expand the portfolio's understanding about particular customer groups, and also to obtain a picture of how our services are interacting with other events in peoples' lives. We have collaborated with external providers in conducting the research that has been the basis for the development of five detailed customer journeys. And these journeys are being rolled out across the portfolio.

One of the key insights that we have gained is that customers' journeys start long before we encounter them. In fact, customers are often not an individual; rather, they are part of a collective, a family. Additionally, they are relying on third parties, other organisations, to find out information, even before they come to us. Often when they come into our organisations, because of the way we currently organise and deliver our services, they are shoehorned into a particular program which might not necessarily meet all of their needs. This last finding is consistent with other research about customers wanting programs to be personal to them.

Another finding is that citizens, depending on what is happening in their lives and on how a service may or may not be delivered to them at a particular point, can fall into a particular life pattern. If DHS is able to recognise some of the trigger points or turning points in a life pattern, we may be able to achieve better outcomes for individuals by proactively reaching out to them.

The insights provided by the customer journeys have been enhanced in Victoria by information derived from 'community conversations'. The value of these conversastions lies in the opportunity to gather a community together to focus on DHS initiatives and how stakeholders can take responsibility for improving service delivery in their community.

We have also thought about the challenges in implementing our vision of co-design. Principally, they are about indentifying the opportunities for doing this detailed design work. Often in government, ideas arise quickly, sometimes influenced by the 24-hour media cycle. But, we must have the vision to look beyond this to determine how we can best pursue the notion of co-design to shape new initiatives, programs and policies for the future.

Jo Sammut: My contribution to this volume concerns a case study of a social program called Building Stronger Communities that was delivered in the Sydney suburb of Macquarie Fields, largely by Housing New South Wales. Accordingly, my contribution concerns not the design of a policy, but the implementation of it in the community.

Macquarie Fields, for most Australians, is known primarily as the site of a riot between residents and police in 2005. It is essentially an estate situated within a suburb, located 13 kilometres outside Campbelltown. It is a mixed, multicultural community, and many of its residents associate more with the Liverpool Local Government Association (LGA) than the Campbelltown LGA because Liverpool is closer.

The public housing sector, which is the principal demographic of Macquarie Fields, is characterised by socio-economic disadvantage. Prior to 2010, when Building Stronger Communities was implemented in Macquarie Fields, the school retention rate was low and the crime rate was high. Since 2010, improvements in both areas have been attributed to the success of Building Stronger Communities.

Instituting this change was not an easy task. Critical to the success of the project was having a small team of three visionaries who were able to lead and implement it. We were not alone, but we had to see past what everybody else was thinking — and saying — to remain objective.

The Building Stronger Communities strategy resulted in practical changes, not only to our citizen engagement processes but also to the entire system of work performed by Housing New South Wales. The six sites that the project encompassed across New South Wales are currently being evaluated and, hopefully, some of the findings that are obtained through this process will benefit future strategy planning, public consultation and engagement for Housing New South Wales estates.

It has been written elsewhere in this volume that we must tailor engagement processes to sectors of the community — one model does not fit all — and that is what we managed to do with this particular strategy.

So what is Building Stronger Communities? In 2007 the then NSW premier, Morris Iemma, announced the strategy, to be led by Housing New South Wales, which was selected to lead the strategy because the common client group — or the common community — lived in social housing. The strategy was an investment of $66 million — not just in Macquarie Fields, but across the state. The aim was to reduce the gap between disadvantaged public housing neighbourhoods and the surrounding neighbourhoods by getting the NGO sector, government, and business to work with the community.

That sounds fantastic, doesn't it? And could you imagine trying to do that in four years? We not only had to imagine it — we had to deliver it. The challenge was that Macquarie Fields at this time was a disengaged community that had had a government intervention following the social disturbance there in 2005. The community and the local NGOs were disillusioned with government — local, state, or federal. And the interventions were not only coming from the state government, but also from the federal government (the National Action Plan, a federal government initiative, was a response to social disturbances in Cronulla, Lakemba and Macquarie Fields).

Hence, a community that felt vulnerable — but which was resilient — suddenly found itself flooded with various government interventions. If this were not challenging enough, our mandate in instituting the strategy involved engaging the community, the NGO sector, other government departments at local and state level, and our own Department of Housing. To us this was like having a polar attraction. The Department of Housing functions predominately as a manager; they are landlords, they manage tenants, and the agency's frontline staff generally had to deal with things like rental arrears, vacancies, noise, nuisance and annoyance, and a variety of personal issues they term as the 'fluffy' ones. For such an agency to deliver such a different sort of program was inevitably going to be a challenge.

There were often tensions between what we were trying to deliver — which was a government initiative — and the day-to-day work of the Department of Housing. This tension was exacerbated because the area had a high incidence of rental arrears. We had to do substantial marketing and communication to convince our colleagues and our clients to partcipate in the program.

Because of these challenges, we were forced to think innovatively in order to successfully implement the strategy. But, while we did this, we were hampered by political constraints. We had to deliver the program within four years and develop a Regeneration Partnership Plan that would be implemented by our partner government agencies, the NGOs, and the community.

For these reasons we often termed it 'the four year "speed dating" process' (although we did receive a six-month extension), and looked longingly to Victoria and Queensland, which both had eight years to do this sort of work.

And yet, we wanted to make sure this was a sustainable process. To build sustainability, one of our key focuses over the four years was to get citizens to recognise the short period of time available in which to make a change and that it would be necessary for them to carry on the mandate after our program had concluded. We wanted them to refashion and update the program because the priorities for the residents of Macquarie Fields are constantly changing.

We tried to build this desire for sustainability into the core business plan of the department and into its day-to-day responsibilities. But tensions remained because, even though some of the Department's policy supported our aims, the agency had another mandate, concerning their role as landlords and delivering associated services.

We made the Department responsible for particular areas of the strategy in Macquarie Fields, usually involving the physical infrastructure, such as the service specifications, building capacities, and funding arrangements. This meant that other services that were important for the regeneration plan would be delivered through other means and networks.

One of the first things we did was to get involved with other programs in the community, so as to establish a presence. We knew that we would face much cynicism, such was the fly-in, fly-out nature of previous efforts of these kinds.

We were honest from the outset, however, and said: 'We're only here for four years; this is what we have to work with; this is the timeframe; we want you to come along, we need you to come along, it's your community. At the end of the day we go home, you stay'. We took the same honest approach with the other agencies with which we worked.

Our next step was to form a Regeneration Planning Working Group, which was made up of representatives from government, NGOs, businesses and the community. The key focus of this group was the community engagement strategy.

Let me now outline the community visioning process that we underwent. Our planning process was six weeks. We then had eight weeks to collect community data. We were apprehensive about this, because we were convinced not only that the people of Macquarie Fields were sick of being consulted with, but also that there is enough data out there.

But, what we wanted was to hear people's responses. We wanted to get a feel for the area. We had enough Australian Bureau of Statistics, census and government data; what we needed instead was to consult with preschool and primary school students, churchgoers and teenagers. This, we felt, would give us a clearer picture of the demographics and particular needs in the area. To give you an idea of just how thorough we were in this endeavour, we even conducted surveys at the local pub.

Through the planning group, several working groups were formed, one of which was tailored for the strong and vibrant Indigenous community of Macquarie Fields. By doing this we wanted to make sure that the way the consultation would happen with each group would meet that group's needs.

We had a children's working party which explored the issue of how to engage with children, and we used paintings and drawings to do this (questions were created for kids so that they could answer them in these two mediums). With local primary school students, we also developed a poster outlining what they liked in Macquarie Fields, and what else they would like. When I look at that poster today, I see all the elements that we delivered in the regeneration plan. That in itself speaks volumes; it could very well be the poster for the regeneration partnership.

The poster had two sides: one depicting good elements about the community bike parks, skate parks and equipment; and the other showing the bad aspects rubbish, bullies, broken glass and needles. The children of one kindergarten class in the community made a DVD in which they portrayed what they liked about their community.

We also used the creative responses of the children to improve our engagement with the rest of the community. We collected the children's artwork and turned it into a calendar and art books, and included comments from the children. For example, one child said, 'If we get it done now it will be a better place'. The preschool kids developed the Christmas cards that became the official Christmas cards for the south-west region of the Department of Housing.

Our engagement processes targeted the broad community, community leaders, the NGOs, and the other government agencies. Each of these groups responded to surveys, findings and focus groups. From the findings of those engagement processes, we developed popular fact sheets, which included material designed by local children.

Additionally, around 1000 children's art books were produced. With the help of the private sector, we distributed these books to three local schools, and they were used as part of the schools' art classes.

From all the consultation that we undertook, we then formed what we called the implementation group to put in place key early intervention and prevention strategies. These included a focus on youth, as this demographic had been particularly neglected in Macquarie Fields in terms of the coordination between services. Young people told us that they wanted better service coordination. We managed to achieve this by ensuring that we had input into the specifications of services that were funded through the Department of Community Services.

Another important aspect of the regeneration partnership was its reporting mechanism. This was done quarterly as part of our four-year evaluation strategy, with reporting mandatory for each of the leading workgroups, the other government agencies and NGOs. In this way they were accountable to the Regeneration Partnership Plan, and they had to report against a template. The reason we did that was to make clear that this was not a Housing New South Wales Partnership Plan; it was a Regeneration Partnership Plan of all the agencies, the community, and the other service providers in the area.

Our goal of shifting peoples' assumption that this was a Housing New South Wales initiative required continuous community consultation as well as changes to our internal structures. We were fortunate that the team leader of the local office was engaged in community development, and was people-focused, rather than arrears-focused. The team leader was also respected by the community in Macquarie Fields — something that is novel in a housing estate. He was able to transfer some of this community respect to his team, to the benefit of the entire project.

Our community consultation succeeded because of our flexibility: we did it anytime and anywhere. And, if a particular approach didn't work, we tried something different. When one street, for example, was letterbox-dropped a few days before a meeting about upgrading a nearby park, we noticed no one was collecting the letter. So instead we raised awareness of the project by doorknocking on a Saturday morning; we succeeded in having people consult with us in their pyjamas, over the bonnets of their cars, at 9 am. We were able to listen to peoples' ideas about their area. Ultimately, these consultations on the upgrade to the park led to the once rubbish-strewn landscape of that area now being regenerated with rockery and trees.

In all the strategies we undertook we had a 'give back' policy: if we were serious about changing the public space, we had to incorporate all members of the community. For example we invited some former graffiti taggers in the area to be involved in murals we called 'community arts' (the local council would not allow us to call it 'graffiti art'). We were able to get them on board through consultation strategies encompassing community leaders, local teams, youth services and other government level agencies.

But this whole project was no smooth road; in nearly everything we did, we encountered resistance. But we also had resilient staff who were intent on including those around them in this endeavour.

An example of community resistance was seen in a particular park in Macquarie Fields that had previously only been used once or twice a year. We wanted to upgrade it to make it a hub for the community. But, when we went out to talk to people about this park, though they had some great ideas, they wanted to see a six foot fence surrounding the whole area and somebody holding the key. The perception was that if anything was done in Macquarie Fields it would just be destroyed within a couple of days.

And it was our team that was saying, 'No, no, no, we'll put all these things in place with the community, and you will be part of the process.' And it was. The community led this process, and eventually sent leaders of the Indigenous community of Macquarie Fields to inspect different community parks across Sydney; after this, they drew basic designs for their ideal park.

That initial design stayed largely intact — there were only a few minor changes from the landscape architects. The community stayed involved by painting the 'snake trail', which became a bike trail and an exercise station circuit. It also made an appearance on the SBS gardening and lifestyle programme *Costa's Garden*, such was the success of the community engagement — and ownership — that led to the creation of this park.

These projects also served to bridge a gap within the community. Pupils from both local schools grew gardens together and helped to plant trees in the park's eucalyptus reserve. Previously, even though they were located less than 400-metres apart, the two schools had had little collaboration with one another and had only communicated when they had to transfer students from one school to the other.

All of this was achieved because of the community engagement and capacity building processes that we had developed. We may have been the ones driving the project, but there were many others who came on board and helped achieve its end.

Having succeeded in the community engagement and capacity building goals of the Regeneration Plan, we moved to the transition phase, in which we handed over responsibility to the community for the ongoing project tasks. These tasks included graffiti eradication, rubbish removal, and redevelopment of public spaces. As the first part of our exit strategy, we conducted in September 2010 one final consultation with the community, this time using a new online survey system called Survey Monkey. As part of that process, we developed a transition plan and made other parts of other government agencies, NGOs, and the community responsible for delivering parts of it. We also utilised the internet to ask the community what changes they had seen since we began working with them. This was an extension of a community visioning exercise that we had undertaken five years beforehand, in which we asked people what they wanted Macquarie Fields to resemble in five years.

I predict that some of the project will drop off because the community in particular cannot be held accountable like we can; however, for now at least, much of the project is being followed through. The challenge will be whether the governance structures remain in place, because it is the governance structures that manage that whole implementation of the transition plan.

19. Dilemmas of Engagement: Seriously empowering our community

Deb Symons

In my contribution to this volume I will analyse Victoria's approach to engaging with the communities affected by the 2009 'Black Saturday' bushfires. In the aftermath of the bushfires, the approach was taken to put communities at the centre of planning and decision-making, and to work extensively with them to develop recovery plans and to include their input into local government plans for the future.

Following the devastating bushfires in Victoria in February 2009, an unprecedented recovery effort was required and included the establishment of the Victoria Bushfire Reconstruction and Recovery Authority (VBRRA). The fires affected over 70 communities in diverse areas of Victoria and saw:

- over 2000 homes lost
- approximately 2000 homes seriously damaged
- a broad range of community infrastructure damaged or lost, including several schools and halls
- significant losses to business
- the loss of over 8000 livestock and an estimated 12,500 km of fencing
- the loss of an estimated 1,000,000 native animals
- most tragically, the loss of 173 lives.

Approach to community engagement

I joined the VBRRA in its first weeks and soon found myself managing the community engagement team, with community-led recovery as the central tenet of the organisation's recovery strategy.

It is important to stress the diversity of communities affected by the bushfires. While many people know of the suffering endured by communities such as Marysville and Kinglake, there were in fact over 70 communities across Victoria affected by the bushfires, with fire services responding to over 500 events in a single day.

The point of the above statistics is not to dwell on the detail of the fires and their impact but to highlight that our engagement, from the outset, had to recognise that the people we were to work with were devastated in so many aspects of their lives — be that through personal loss, loss of their home and security, loss of neighbours and friends, loss of income or employment, loss of livestock and long-held farming property, or loss of community.

Some areas were devastated. Moreover, they were often close to the urban fringe — Kinglake West is the most well-known example. The significance of this is that many people did not appreciate the risks inherent in the environment within which they lived, as they were so close to 'town'.

Community led recovery

A range of research tells us that communities recover best when they are enabled to participate and lead in their own recovery. Briefly, VBRRA's approach to the community-led recovery consisted of:

- VBRRA, in conjunction with many local government areas, supported the establishment of 33 Community Recovery Committees (CRCs) across Victoria.
- The members of each CRC were 'regular' community members, not organisation representatives.
- Each CRC was asked to prepare a community recovery plan with, and on behalf of, their community. They did this over several months, typically via workshops and planning days.
- In total, the 33 CRCs presented to government over 1100 recovery projects in their plans.
- A team of community engagement coordinators worked closely with CRCs and the wider community to engage, develop and nurture community participation and community confidence in undertaking their own local planning and decision-making.

As this was not the first such disaster experienced in Australia, a history of good practice, methodology and approach to recovery was available to be drawn on. The Victorian scenario, though, did have some unique elements to it, most notably the number of different communities affected. As a newly formed organisation, the VBRRA was also something of an unknown and none of the documented arrangements for state recovery included this entity; nonetheless the VBRRA was entrusted with coordinating and leading the recovery. To do this, it was necessary to work with all state government departments, several federal government departments, the Australian Defence Force and over 20 local governments.

While CRCs were given only a single-line mention in the state's Emergency Management Manual, the VBRRA extended and formalised the concept and pushed for the formation of such committees across all of the communities affected by the bushfires. We also insisted that the CRCs be populated by 'regular' community members, despite many local governments initially preferring to fill them with representative of community groups, such as the Salvation Army and the Red Cross, who were assisting the bushfire recovery effort. It was evident that more direct engagement was necessary.

Each group formed in a different manner, based upon the characteristics of its community. Some communities held formal elections, others nominated people during a community meeting in the local hall, and others used local council support to call for nominations to form a committee.

The experience of the aftermath of the 'Black Saturday' bushfires reveals the dilemmas arising from attempts to seriously engage and empower communities. The following eight points encapsulate these dilemmas.

Seriously empowering communities: A short list of complexities and dilemmas

The greatest challenge of effective community engagement is that, put simply, it is the more difficult road to take. It requires:

- Senior and strong leadership backing this kind of approach is necessary for success.
- Leaders and policy-makers should be willing to have decisions that are not just supported by communities but also shaped by them. Be wary of false engagement strategies.
- Community members are not employees. As a group, they are unlikely to behave in a compliant or skilled fashion. Your skills as a facilitator, negotiator and arbitrator are critical.
- Engaging the community will lengthen the time required to make decisions. Other elements of your program need to recognise this.
- You can expect projects to cost more, not less, following community engagement.
- The community is likely to ask government to do 'non-governmental' things.
- Community engagement is not about efficiency. It is about the long-term health of communities, and recognition of the value of community spirit.
- In a world driven by Key Performance Indicators (KPIs), successful community engagement is hard to measure.

1. I would suggest that with engagement if you do not have senior and strong leadership that 'gets it' and really 'wants it', then just don't do it. We were fortunate we had good leaders who sponsored engagement, became deeply involved in the process themselves and often intervened on decisions which had lacked engagement or were racing ahead without waiting for the community. There were plenty of people who did not support or agree with our approach, many of them senior leaders and decision-makers themselves. If we had not had the senior backing that we did with our approach, the whole thing would probably have been more damaging for communities than helpful, as it certainly raised expectations that required us to deliver upon regularly. Hence, engagement needs senior and strong leadership that understands and wants to engage with the community. This is essential for the success of such a program. Without the support of strong leadership in meeting the expectations of the communities, the VBRRA program would have been unsuccessful.

2. Engagement of this nature must inform and shape policy or service delivery decisions. Effective communication that allows communities to shape decisions is the basis of this form of engagement. While the VBRRA program received some eccentric and radical requests, on the whole the communities understood and expressed what they needed better than the administrators, and were happy to argue their point, negotiate their needs, and listen to the challenges faced in meeting their needs.

3. One of the challenges of engaging directly with community members is the diversity of individuals who find a voice as members of committees. Some of the people in the communities and on the CRCs were traumatised by the bushfires; some had trouble communicating; some could not remember the discussion and decisions of the week before. Many had never been involved in community committees or workshops or acted as representatives of their community, and they were not obliged to behave in a particular way. Community engagement does not always follow an orderly, well-paced, focused and necessarily respectful process. That said, I am proud of the lasting investment that we have made in these communities. Through the committees and ongoing activities and projects that were established, we can be certain that there is a much greater capacity and capability in these communities to form and run local committees now.

4. Related to the point above, but important as a distinct issue, it is critical to recognise that engaging with communities will almost certainly extend a project's timeline. Engagement is rarely something that can be done quickly, and it certainly is not something that can be rolled out towards the end of a program. People focused on community engagement have an important role

in influencing others to ensure that the engagement strategy addresses the broad and specific aspects of the project, from the onset if possible.

5. Engagement will often result in greater costs rather than any cost savings, largely through an approach to negotiate with and learn from communities. The negotiation process might mean that government can deliver what it needs to, but it may have to add elements which assist the community, based on its preferences. For example, the VBRRA placed temporary health services in a number of communities; as we worked with communities and listened to them tell us what they needed, the range of services and the timeframes for which they were offered were extended. Thus, even though the visitation statistics did not highlight a need for the services, the communities convinced the VBRRA that this was due to lack of awareness of and comfort with these services, rather than lack of need for them. As a consequence, evening and weekend sessions on mental health first aid were held to make people feel comfortable about using the services.

6. The VBRRA was regularly asked to look into areas which did not fall within the purview of a government agency. The bushfire recovery process is an extreme case study, but communities came to see the VBRRA as a central coordinator for everything, not just for government services. As a result it became involved in events and projects outside its core business. The benefits of such engagement were clear: it built trust, rapport and respect necessary in the tense atmosphere in these ravaged communities. One example of this occurred in Marysville. After it became apparent that many of the landlords or owners along the main street were not in a position to re-establish their shops at the time, the community lobbied furiously for the government to buy one of the only standing buildings — a former car museum — and to fit out this building so that the supermarket could return. While governments are not usually in the business of purchasing commercial real estate, fitting it out for retail use and setting up a body corporate, in this instance such an approach was needed. It was a lengthy process — and the VBRRA was criticised by the community for not listening and for taking too long — but, in the end, their voices were heard and made a difference.

7. Engagement is not something that facilitates compliance responsibilities, nor does it drive efficiency.

8. It is not possible to consider the dilemmas of engagement without mentioning 'success'. Measuring the outcomes of engagement with communities is hard to do. It is important to define success for engagement activities early in the process, however, long-term evaluation is also crucial. There is also the issue of what defines 'value', not just for a particular project, but for community health more generally. Single department approaches are unable to adequately

account for this. Perhaps this is a challenge for the public sector to consider, as we are all contributing to community health in our own ways.

Ongoing discussions and debates

- Is there a genuine sponsorship of community engagement at the highest level of government?
- Are there tangible positive outcomes? How are they measured?
- Are we prepared to empower citizens or do we just want them to publicly agree with us?

Part V. Case Studies: Engaging with information technology and new media

20. Volunteers as Agents of Co-production: 'Mud armies' in emergency services

Fiona Rafter

My department, Queensland's Department of Community Safety, is a merger of Emergency Services and the former Department of Corrective Services. The department includes Emergency Management Queensland and the Fire and Ambulance Service. In my contribution to this volume I will share what I believe to be a successful case of the use of social media for the purposes of community engagement, albeit set amidst the most devastating series of natural disasters to affect the state of Queensland. It has provided an opportunity for our department and government to rethink the way we engage with the public, build resilience in communities and mobilise volunteers.

Between November 2010 and April 2011 Queensland was struck by a series of natural disasters. Extensive flooding caused by periods of heavy rainfall, destruction caused by a number of storm cells — including cyclones Tasha, Anthony and Yasi — and subsequent monsoonal flooding, resulted in the state of Queensland being declared as disaster-affected. The extreme weather conditions that Queensland experienced saw extensive, sequential natural disasters that resulted in lives being lost and unprecedented widespread devastation.

During December 2010, southern and central Queensland, including the cities of Bundaberg and Rockhampton, were most affected by the rain depression resulting from Cyclone Tasha. During this time, Rockhampton, Queensland's eighth-biggest population centre, was inaccessible to the rest of the state by air, road or rail.

In January 2011, south-east Queensland was affected by riverine and flash flooding. Toowoomba, especially, had significant flash flooding in its main street. Several people lost their lives, including a mother and her teenage son, who were swept away while driving a car down Toowoomba's main street. Even after the floodwaters had subsided, there was substantial infrastructure damage in and around the city.

However, Grantham and the Lockyer Valley were the most significantly affected by flooding. This region experienced what was later described as an 'inland tsunami' that washed away cars, houses and people with devastating force. Moreover, it happened too fast for the townspeople to react.

Ipswich also experienced a severe case of riverine flooding. The banks of the Bremer River broke causing the main street to be inundated with water. The top of a large supermarket building barely poked out of the water, while a shark was seen swimming in floodwaters nearby. As with elsewhere in the state, people were killed in Ipswich. Mostly, this was because they dared to enter the water and were swept away as a result. Sometimes people were trapped because they did not realise roads had been cut off. There were mass evacuations in Ipswich, with thousands of people affected.

In Brisbane, riverside suburbs and the CBD were inundated with water when the Brisbane River broke its banks. Brisbane's experience was different from the regional centres because its residents received plenty of warning about the flash flooding. Nonetheless, there were mass evacuations and there was no power or transport in the CBD. Homes and businesses were badly damaged and the commercial zone was essentially closed for weeks. Suncorp Stadium, the city's iconic rugby league and soccer stadium, was turned into a muddy swimming pool; Southbank, one of Brisbane's chief tourist attractions, was inundated with water.

In February 2011, north and far north Queensland were hit by category five Cyclone Yasi, which made landfall near Cardwell, between Cairns and Townsville. For those who had been in the path of the category five Cyclone Larry at nearby Innisfail in 2006, this second cyclone was particularly cruel.

The impact on Queensland of this series of natural disasters was devastating. By 11 March 2011, all of Queensland was disaster-activated. The majority of the 37 people who had been killed drowned in flash flooding. All 73 local government areas and over 210 communities were affected. Helicopters evacuated the 314 residents from the town of Theodore; the entire townships of Cardwell and Condamine were evacuated – twice each. Condamine had to be evacuated for a second time after it experienced a second flood, while Cardwell was evacuated first due to the cyclone and then because of the flood.

In total, there were 360 swift water rescues that took place from the floodwaters, 10,500 people had to be housed in evacuation centres as Cyclone Yasi struck, and 480,000 homes and businesses were affected, including 136,000 residential properties. Over 9000 kilometres of roads were damaged and nearly 5000 kilometres of the rail network was affected. Finally, 122,000 insurance claims have been lodged at an estimated cost of $3.6 billion.

The importance of resilience

Extreme weather conditions have always been a feature of the Australian climate and, in Queensland, floods and cyclones pose the greatest threat. For that reason, disaster management has moved away from the traditional approach, which focused on response to natural disasters by our emergency services, to one focusing on resilience and shared responsibility by all sectors of the community and government to prevent and mitigate disasters.

The Council of Australian Governments (COAG) has said in its Natural Disaster Resilience Statement that resilience is 'the capacity to prevent, mitigate, prepare for, respond to and recover from the impacts of disasters'. Importantly, the statement also recognises the fundamental role that volunteers play in building community resilience. One of its priorities, therefore, is to provide ongoing support for the recruitment, retention, training, equipping and maintaining of unpaid support — a key priority in Queensland, particularly because of our reliance on disaster management volunteers.

COAG has also outlined its desire to make volunteering easier. This concern was first raised in 2009 in the aftermath of Cyclone Larry in North Queensland. As a result, there is work currently being done at a national level on what is called the 'volunteer passport'. This would make it easier for people to volunteer and to work across the different volunteer organisations.

The State Emergency Service (SES) in Queensland, the organisation usually responsible for being first on the ground when a disaster strikes (particularly in the remote and regional areas of the state), is a voluntary organisation. And, although Emergency Management Queensland provides the SES with some administration support, the service, which consists of nearly 7000 volunteers based in 342 groups across Queensland, remains unpaid. The Rural Fire Service, which performs the role of first responders at disaster events to evaluate what is required on the ground, is also a predominantly volunteer organisation. There are 34,000 firefighting volunteers and approximately 1500 rural fire brigades across Queensland.

Queensland is a vast state and its communities rely on these volunteers for disaster management preparedness and response. It is a model that has served the state well, even if there have been challenges with attracting and retaining volunteers — although Queensland is not alone in this regard. There has been much research conducted into this problem, with the five major challenges in attracting, supporting and retaining emergency management volunteers identified as being: time, training, cost, recognition and the commitment of volunteer people. An additional problem is the fact that many volunteers are ageing, and young volunteers use volunteering as a pathway to paid employment, so they remain in their roles only for short periods of time.

It is no surprise to learn that bureaucracy and culture also pose an additional challenge or barrier to recruiting volunteers. In Community Safety, for example, employees must fulfil separate criteria to volunteer for the different agencies. Bureaucracy can be seen as putting up barriers, rather than promoting the volunteering process. National and international evidence points to the fact that programs that demonstrate success in volunteer recruitment focus on removing barriers by providing flexible approaches to volunteering, providing the right tools to do the right job, making training flexible and covering out-of-pocket expenses.

A success story: Spontaneous volunteering in response to Brisbane's floods

In response to the Brisbane floods, the wider community was desperate to help those in need. And, because there was advanced warning in Brisbane, people began to help others before the floods arrived. The community's desire to provide assistance, however, was even more evident after the waters subsided and individuals and businesses wanted to know what they could do to help victims of the flood. The Brisbane City Council, through its Facebook site, issued a call to action on the weekends of 15–16 January and 22–23 January. The council established four volunteer coordination centres in Brisbane and volunteers at these centres were then transported by council buses to their allocated sectors.

Volunteers were asked to bring a bucket, spade, boots, sunscreen and hat. Gumboots sold out in Brisbane on the first day of the call to action and 23,000 volunteers were registered at those four centres. The response was so overwhelming that some people were turned away. I know people that drove from the Gold Coast with their bucket, spade and boots only to be told there was no more room. In addition to those who attended and registered at the coordination centres, there were also many other people who were volunteering informally. These informal engagements were often facilitated through social media.

The Brisbane City Council believes that, as a result of its call to action, between 50,000 and 60,000 people volunteered across the weekend of January 15–16 and a significant number again on the following weekend. This overwhelming community response and volunteering effort has never been experienced before. So, how did it happen and what opportunities does it present? Firstly, social media and crisis communication played a significant role in information dissemination during and after the flood crisis. Social media provided the most up-to-date information from and to the community and enabled contact between government, family and friends; it mobilised entire communities into what would be dubbed the 'mud army'. The worldwide level of interest and support created an emotional response.

One positive aftermath of the Queensland floods, and indeed of the series of natural disasters that have struck Australia in recent summers, is that there is now a platform in place to quickly mobilise volunteer disaster response teams. In Queensland, as in the rest of the country, when the disaster management framework is triggered, the police may take over the primary response role; ultimately, though, it is a multi-layered response. Local government is at the heart of this, because local knowledge is critical to successfully preparing for and responding to a natural disaster.

Consequently, when a disaster occurs, the local government works in collaboration with the Commonwealth and defence — all of which played a significant role in the response to the 2011 Queensland floods. In addition to the three tiers of government, volunteer organisations work collaboratively and across jurisdictions; Victoria and New South Wales sent both paid officers and volunteers to Queensland to help with the floods, a favour returned by Queensland when Victoria experienced floods of its own later in 2011.

How did the Queensland government use social media and what opportunities do we have to use it in the future? The Queensland Police Service (QPS) used Facebook, Twitter and YouTube for the first time during the floods, with effective results in disseminating accurate information and debunking myths, such as the need to stockpile food. This helped to restore calm and order when — particularly in shopping centres — people were beginning to panic. The QPS Facebook page had 39 million hits during the floods and became a reference point for all crisis-related information through its photos, live streaming and video media conferences, many of which were conducted jointly with Premier Anna Bligh. The Facebook page received its highest level of traffic on 10 January 2011 during a video address from the premier and the police commissioner.

Additionally, a Queensland Floods iPhone application was developed by the QPS, which had successful results. Given the urgency of the situation, the application was developed quickly and outside the QPS's normal approval process. The application allowed the QPS to transmit up-to-date information to the public about which areas to avoid, where to evacuate from, and other related messages and it is likely that its implementation avoided further loss of life.

Will there be future opportunities for social media to be used to mobilise volunteers? Most certainly. In fact, this is something on which Community Safety is currently working. The benefits of social media are obvious: it is free and available 24/7; it offers instant access to information; it uses collaboration or 'crowd sourcing' to ensure the information is up-to-date (taking into account the inaccuracy of some information) and it is regarded as a legitimate source of information. It can be accessed without power (most of Queensland didn't have power for a significant period of time during the floods) and it can build community support for people willing to receive and respond to messages.

Social media complements, rather than replaces, the traditional media, as is clear from traditional broadcast media's use of social media to supplement their own research.

Having said that, I think it is clear that there will always be a need for more traditional volunteers in disaster zones. Such people make a commitment to join an organisation and, in order to carry out their tasks, must undergo specific training. This costs money: $4000 per person, according to our calculations. While traditional volunteers will remain the backbone of Queensland's disaster management force, it is critical, however, to take advantage of the opportunities that social media, in particular, presents in increasing the numbers of traditional volunteers and supplementing them with spontaneous volunteers like the 'mud army'. The 'mud army', as Gerry Stoker (Chapter 2) would say, is evidence that sometimes all that people need to become engaged in their community is a nudge.

21. Informing Tax Policy Legislation: Thinking differently about consultation processes

Mary Craig

The phrase 'tax policy' does not usually elicit wild excitement in the general public. So, for fear of disengaging readers of this volume with a long presentation on a dry topic, my contribution will briefly use the field of tax policy to explore the new dimensions of community consultation. Together with Gail Kelly (Chapter 22), I will particularly explore the use of online forums for engaging citizens on tax policy. I am not, however, going to pretend that this is a transformational use of a piece of technology. I note that Martin Stewart-Weeks (Chapter 9) covers many of these aspects in his earlier chapter. Nonetheless, new technology has greatly assisted Inland Revenue in New Zealand to engage more people in the formation of tax policy than could have been achieved with traditional methods. The success of these new approaches to citizen engagement has encouraged our organisation specifically to investigate other new technologies which could our improve citizen engagement methods and, more broadly, to look at things differently and take risks.

This contribution will provide some background to the new citizen engagement approaches adopted by New Zealand's Inland Revenue organisation before Kelly elaborates on the experiences and effects of these changes.

We all know that citizens have a legal obligation to comply with tax legislation, as with other legislation. At Inland Revenue we have tried hard to make it easy for people to comply with tax legislation, whether it is via the service delivery interface, or to comply with the new or established policies that we administer. In New Zealand there is now an extensive formal legislative consultation process in place and it is prescribed and very detailed. Any new legislation or any significant change to legislation must be put out to the general public for consultation and comment. This has been done in the past through traditional means and we would generally have about 10 such consultations each year.

The responses that we get from these consultations helps us frame the legislation, as well as flagging any associated issues that may be of interest, whether they are innocuous or contentious, or whether they merely highlight emerging trends or problems in which the government of the day may be interested.

There is no doubt though, that these traditional consultations are long, complicated processes and sometimes expensive in time and resources. The consultation documents that we publish range between 30 to 60 pages in length, sometimes longer, and usually what we get back, in kind, are similar length documents. They are almost invariably detailed text-based documents. We will accept submissions or comments by post or by email, and sometimes they are written by hand. This is the standard consultation process for tax legislation that has prevailed for some time. It connects principally with the 'usual suspects', with whom we regularly consult and, in most cases, we can anticipate their views.

Having said that, there are still a whole range of other activities and functions that our organisation undertakes that are not strictly about tax policy. While tax policy constitutes around 50 per cent of Inland Revenue's work, we also have service delivery obligations, whether they concern student loans, or working out tax credits for families. In addition, we administer KiwiSaver — New Zealand's state-run retirement fund scheme — and child support payments.

But, to return to the theme of this presentation, the problems with the standard consultation process have become evident and Inland Revenue has begun to seek to go beyond the traditional limited approach. Feedback on tax policy changes tended to be generalised or 'chunked up' and submitted by a third party. In Inland Revenue, we wanted to begin to engage those people who do not typically provide feedback about changes in tax legislation. Such citizens tend to hold individual views, rather than those representing a particular association or interest group or demographic. Consequently, what we were looking for in terms of feedback and consultation were individual inputs and responses.

An obvious response to the problem of improving the breadth of consultation was to start thinking about information technology and the fact that Inland Revenue had yet to exploit its potential, other than to receive documents via email. It was clear that that new information technologies presented an exciting variety of ways in which we could consult with people and 'push their buttons' — including through an emphasis on new forms of social media and other forms of technology. The consultation process no longer needed to be confined to text and lengthy documentation. Contemporary information technology could provide a diversity of consultative methods.

Another important advantage in harnessing this new technology is the time that is saved as a consequence. Traditionally, consultations about tax legislation have been lengthy processes; they can take months, sometimes years. But, in utilising online forums, consultation was occurring in real time, or as near to real time as we could possibly get. Consequently, we have now moved to a platform where submitters are talking to each other, commenting on each other's views, as well as talking to us in Inland Revenue, and talking to the government more generally. In this way it is a real conversation. And, although some of this input must be filtered out, we are also getting rich and valuable information — quickly. Thanks to new technology, we are now able to send our information out more quickly and in a manner which is more manageable for both individuals and groups.

22. Inland Revenue New Zealand: From hosting consultations to managing conversations

Gail Kelly

What I am trying to convey in this chapter is that being a tax department, we in Inland Revenue in New Zealand are often bound by secrecy, legislation and risk-averse management, which makes our decision to seek feedback online a bold step for us.

To date, we have undertaken three online consultations, each with different audiences. In 2009 we worked closely with those to whom we give student loans. As we offer 627,000 student loans, currently totalling $NZ10.8 billion, this represents a significant part of our business. Consequently, we wanted to look at ways that might help to reform and simplify the administration of those student loans and ultimately to get some of that money back into the government coffers so that it could be used on other social programs. But, if we think about the students who receive student loans, it is not a group that is typically riveted by tax policy. Students do, however, embrace the latest technology. We thus ran a moderated online forum for this group over a six week period. As a result, our website received 5600 visits and 120 comments — a much higher usage than usual and clear evidence of our success in engaging the student demographic on this issue.

The second consultation we conducted aimed to investigate and simplify the general administration processes of the tax system. Again, we held an online forum. Our website received 10,000 visits and 1000 votes on different types of policy proposals. We also used short videos on our website to illustrate how life was before and how it would be after the policy changes. These videos were written, acted and filmed in-house, exposing some hidden talent in Inland Revenue.

We also used Facebook as a medium to give ongoing publicity to the forums and we portrayed, through specific examples, the impact that our proposed changes would have on businesses, individuals, software developers and not-for-profit organisations.

The third online consultation we undertook was our Child Support Online Survey. For this we received over 2000 submissions and tens of thousands of comments. Our respondents spent approximately three and a half minutes reading and digesting each page of our consultation document. Given our child support customers generally have an emotional investment in the issues involved, it makes sense that they would take the time to give feedback on the changes that would affect them.

Overall, the comments that we received were positive. The central question for us, however, was whether this new form of consultation was more effective than our previous consultations, which used traditional techniques? Unfortunately, this question was difficult to answer because in every policy consultation we ask the public about different elements of a wide range of legislation. Some proposed legislation maybe straightforward and other legislation contentious. Often, then, the legislation itself influences the public's response, more than the medium of consultation. We will therefore have to assess different consultation methods on the same area of legislation in order to better understand the efficacy of our new consultation techniques.

What has become clear is that online consultations have given the public greater opportunity to comment on the tax policy issues that matter to them. Whereas our traditional consultations were characterised by our agency dominating the agenda, online consultations more closely resemble a conversation between two equal parties.

We believe this 'conversation' approach generates different types of outcomes. It has introduced to Inland Revenue a wider range of perspectives and shown us different ways of looking at things. Most importantly, this approach is more flexible insofar as it provides the public with a forum in which they feel comfortable providing comment on parts of the legislation rather than one in which they feel obligated to be aware of all of it.

So where are we at now? Well, we are considering extending our social media consultation to include Twitter, Facebook, YouTube and mobile technology. Going forward for us, however, the big question will be: what do people want from their tax administration and how much do they want to interact with us? Will individuals appreciate the engagement or resent the intrusion? We have opened up new channels of consultation to be managed into the future — so will the prevailing feeling be that wider voices are being heard or more annoyance for those that treasure their privacy. Do taxpayers, students and families want tax administrators popping up on their personal technology? Only time will tell how these new forms of consultation will play out with the public.

www.ingramcontent.com/pod-product-compliance
Lightning Source LLC
Chambersburg PA
CBHW061245270326

41928CB00041B/3428